Reigning in the Storm

Favor Campbell

Favor Campbell

Reigning in the Storm
Copyright © 2020 by Favor Campbell

Scriptures marked NLT are taken from the HOLY BIBLE, NEW LIVING TRANSLATION,, Copyright© 1996, 2004, 2007 by Tyndale House Foundation. Used by permission of Tyndale House Publishers, Inc., Carol Stream, Illinois 60188. All rights reserved. Used by permission.

Scriptures marked NIV are taken from THE HOLY BIBLE, NEW INTERNATIONAL VERSION ®. Copyright© 1973, 1978, 1984, 2011 by Biblica, Inc.™. Used by permission of Zondervan.

Scriptures marked ESV are taken THE HOLY BIBLE, ENGLISH STANDARD VERSION ® Copyright© 2001 by Crossway, a publishing ministry of Good News Publishers. Used by permission.

Scriptures marked MSG are taken from THE MESSAGE: THE BIBLE IN CONTEMPORARY ENGLISH, copyright©1993, 1994, 1995, 1996, 2000, 2001, 2002. Used by permission of NavPress Publishing Group.

Published by: Favor Campbell
Cover Design by: C.S. Fritz
Editing by: www.sharmansedits.com
Published in the United States of America
ISBN No. 978-0-578-66609-9

Table of Contents

Favor Campbell

Introduction

Who is like you Lord, God Almighty? You Lord, are mighty and your faithfulness surrounds you. You rule over the surging sea; when its waves mount up, you still them.
– Psalms 89:8-9 (NIV)

The torrential rain and the loud, drum-like sounding booms from the thunder seem like they're never going to end. As you try to quiet your fears and anxiety from this unexpected storm, it seems as if your body is tensing up even more, so much so that you can feel the stress all over. Your neck, shoulders, and even your stomach are in constant discomfort. You look up to the sky trying to see a break somewhere in the clouds. This storm feels like it's lasting forever. Just as soon as the winds subside, they seem to pick right back up again. The rain is starting to fall harder and harder…the winds are blowing louder and louder. It sounds as if the rain is going to break right through the windows. Fear takes over your body and, as much as you try to tell yourself it will be okay, more anxiety creeps in. "WHY? Why is this storm happening now?" you scream out loud to nobody in particular. "I'm not prepared for this, God! When is this storm going to end?" You look out the window and up to the sky again and, through squinted eyes, just when you think you see the sun peeking through the gray clouds, the rain starts all over again.

Does this sound familiar? That rain, that hail, that thunder, and those clouds that all come together to make up nature's storms would all probably seem a lot more bearable than the storm of financial issues, the storm of divorce, the storm of death, the storm of brokenness, the storm of addictions, the storm of infertility, the storm of sickness, the storm of loss, and any other storm you have encountered on this earth.

It's so easy nowadays to compare ourselves to other people who only put their "best" on display. This is one of my grievances with social media. Logging onto any number of social media apps or websites will lead you to believe that you're struggling with your storm alone and that everyone else's life is seemingly perfect. In Socialmedialand, everyone has perfect spouses, perfect kids, perfect hair, several cars, no bills, the perfect vacation, and with this amazing thing called filters, perfect skin! I'm a sociologist, so I'm very intrigued by the personas that many people display when I understand that, more times than not, we all are carrying around the weight of some sort of pain that tends to be covered up by a mask we've been fooled into believing we have to wear.

Growing up in sunny California, I personally did not experience too many intense storms (the weather type) that were so bad that they left a lasting impression on me. At twenty years old, I moved to the east coast and witnessed storms like I had never seen before! I was simply amazed at how hard and fast the rain came out of the sky. Sometimes it would last all day and other times it was literally for just a very short period of time. Every storm is unique.

Your life storm is going to be different than my storm, and my storm is going to be different than the next person's storm. If you get nothing else from this book, please hear what I'm about to say. You are allowed to feel *your* pain without having to compare it to someone else's. This is a book about dealing with YOUR pain. Period. The minute we compare, we hinder our process in healing. Let me explain.

I'll be the first to admit that I've said, "It could always be worse." I haven't lost a child to death, I haven't been involved in a mass shooting, and I haven't been diagnosed with cancer…to name just a few of the major storms of life. So, yes, there are times when I think about my storms and think I may not have a right to feel bad for too long. This happens when I compare. The fact that I don't have a right to feel what I feel is false and as a society, we have to get better at allowing each other to feel our individual pain, no matter what it is. We also have to do better with helping each other through the pain and giving our pain to the One who created us. As a society, we are simultaneously losing our compassion for one another while also moving further away from God — a God who truly loves us and wants to help us. In order to help each other, we must start by helping ourselves first. This is not in a narcissistic or selfish type of way, but in a "God created me therefore I care enough about myself to want better" type of way. This book was written out of the pain from my own storm, but more importantly, out of love to hopefully help you realize you can have victory and ultimately reign in your storm.

We live in a world of clichés and, honestly, I don't like them. I honestly feel as though many people use them out of context (and I admittedly have as well) and, unfortunately, sometimes at the wrong time. During the middle of my storms, I had a revelation about the cliché, "it could always be worse." I've concluded that by making this statement, in essence, we are not allowing ourselves to feel whatever pain we are experiencing in the moment. We're telling ourselves to get over it and to not feel what we feel. Sadness, anger, hurt, frustration, and confusion are all valid human emotions, especially when it seems that life sucker punches us. I've adjusted my thinking to accept that this simple phrase, "it could always be worse," should simply help me not lose sight of my blessings. Simply put, this cliché should remind me of my blessings. We all have something to be grateful for. Knowing and recognizing our blessings **does not** dismiss, nor should it minimize, the storms and trials we are going through. We need to stop comparing our different life storms and be allowed to embrace, feel, and deal with our pain as we need to.

My genuine hope is that we can learn to stop comparing our lives, our problems, and our ability to handle certain situations. Admittedly, I know this is a bit idealistic, especially in the world of social media. Since we all have a different capacity for what we can deal with, it's simply not fair to expect every person to handle a particular situation in a way that we think they should. If we can get to a place where we are allowed to embrace our pain, we can better deal with it and heal from it. The key however, is not to stay in the pain. My hope is that we can start to learn how to compartmentalize embracing and feeling our pain and keep it separate from comparisons with others and the blessings of life.

Another reason I believe we compare our problems with others is to give ourselves permission to stay in the pain. Unfortunately, some of us think that people who wronged us shouldn't have it as "good" as they seemingly do (another comparison). When we look at our problems from the angle of "nobody has gone through what I have gone through," essentially, we're giving ourselves a pass and we're saying we deserve to stay hurt, mad, angry and to stay where we are in the pain. This mindset is the extreme opposite of having victory in your storm.

I'm going to guess that you're reading this book because you want to understand how to get through your pain or your storm. Once we learn to stop comparing and accept OUR individual pain for what it is, we can begin the healing process and learn how to reign in our storm. That, my friend, is my prayer for you and is the purpose of this book. This book was created out of my storm and certain parts were written in the middle of my storm. I learned countless lessons with the biggest being I can reign, or have power, in the middle of my storm. Although not easy, I've allowed my storm to make me a better person and my hope is that I can help someone else, even if just an ounce, move forward through their storm.

I've been thinking of writing a book for quite some time, but couldn't narrow down my topic, which was frustrating me to no end. I felt that between all my life experiences — getting married at twenty years old, moving across the country to live in a place I had never been, struggling through years of infertility, being a stay-at-home mom for ten years, going back to school in my late 20s to finish my bachelor's degree, continuing on and completing my master's degree, not having a relationship with my biological father, competing in fitness competitions, landing my dream
job as a sociology professor...just to name a few — there was some advice I could pass forward to someone. For me, that is what life is about. Being able to help someone who may struggle in the same areas you've already been through. In all of these experiences, I think back and would have loved to pick up a book to give me some insight into the new journey I was embarking on, by choice or not. Unbeknownst to me, God had something for me to write about. I just needed to go through the biggest storm of my life to complete it.

I started to feel a few months prior to beginning this book that I wanted to write about something about going through a storm. I simply just couldn't come up with anything specific enough. Then just like that, in that simple, unexpected moment, I heard from God. The moment I stopped trying so hard was when God placed this topic on my heart. Ironically, I had just finished reading a book with the word "reign" in the title, but it never once dawned on me while reading it that that particular word would be so significant to me. *Reigning in the Storm* is NOT meant to be a preachy book or a "feel good" book. It's meant to be a real book written by a real person, full of imperfections and flaws, that will remind you that no matter what you've gone through, no matter how many imperfections you may feel like you have, no matter what storm you're trying to get through, God LOVES you and will carry you through, just as He has carried me. It's a book to remind you that we ALL go through storms and, because of that, we should always feel comfort in knowing we're not alone. My storms have made me even more compassionate towards others because I personally understand the emotional, spiritual, and sometimes physical pain that can so easily consume you. If you've, however, gone through any storm in life but have felt yourself become more bitter instead of better, I would implore you to strongly consider seek counseling of some sort. Bitterness often results from unresolved issues and. if left unaddressed, can continue to hinder your emotional, spiritual, and physical growth. Remember, asking for help is not a sign of weakness; it's a sign of strength.

I am praying my way through the writing of this book. I want God to guide my words and put on my heart exactly what I need and should share with you.

Through my storms, I wanted nothing more than to just have somebody hear me out and understand my pain. I read as many books as I possibly could just to feel a connection and know that someone else had been where I was and had made it through. We all have experienced different levels of pain. As I mentioned before, we all have a different capacity for what we can handle. God knows this. If you feel like the storm is never going to end, my dear friend, trust me when I say it will. Allow God to help you the way only He can. Proverbs 30:5 (MSG) says, *"Every promise of God proves true; he protects everyone who runs to him for help."*

My goal is to be as transparent, vulnerable, and as genuine as possible, while praying you feel my immense love I have for my Heavenly Father. Not one of us is without our flaws and imperfections, but our flaws and imperfections do not define us. I want you to reread the last sentence, but this time say it out loud and personalize it — "My flaws and imperfections DO NOT define me!" My desire as you read through these pages of this book is that you will truly feel God's loving arms wrapped around you reminding you that He has never left your side. He's always been there and will continue to be there for you...if you allow Him to be. God is a loving God, but He's not a pushy God. There is nothing in this world like the love from our precious Father. I've learned so much in my storm and I continue to learn something new every day. I pray God uses me to help you truly know you CAN Reign in the Storm. God bless you!

Favor Campbell

---Favor ☺

Chapter 1

Tempest

I said, "Oh, that I had the wings of a dove! I would fly away and be at rest. I would flee far away and stay in the desert. I would hurry to my place of shelter, far from the tempest and storm." – Psalms 55:6-8 (NIV)

I thought for about two seconds about entitling this chapter, "Really God?!" But I wanted to keep with the storm analogy (but let me tell you, I was this close!) "Really God?!" is a phrase that entered my mind more times than I could possibly count during the past several years and even currently at times as I write this book. A divorce after sixteen years of marriage. "Really God?!" An unexpected pregnancy and miscarriage a year later after years of struggling with infertility. "Really God?!" An unforeseen major surgery in the middle of all of this. "Really God?!" My ex-husband marrying his former employee almost two years to the day our divorce was final, the co-worker who I knew and who also played a huge role in the demise of our marriage. "REALLY GOD?!" Isn't that how we often feel and the question we often ask when life comes at us with what feels like a ton of bricks?

Tempest isn't a modern-day term we hear too often unless it's in the context of the Shakespeare

14

play and even then, that play may not be as commonly known as such classics like Romeo and Juliet, Hamlet, or Macbeth. The power and definition of the word "tempest" is so strong there was nothing more appropriate to name this chapter. A tempest is a violent storm, especially one that consists of rain, hail, or snow. This book is not about nature's violent storms, but it is about the storms of life that often hit us unexpectedly.

I'm assuming there has been or there is currently a storm in your life that you're desperately trying to understand and get through. If you're currently not in the middle of a storm, I pray this book will be a good resource for someone you know who is, or it will benefit you later on in life during a tough time.

Let's first talk about what I'm referring to when I use the word storm. If you look up the definition of a storm, there's a variety of responses. The definitions that I liked that really sum up what I'm referencing when I talk about a storm are, "a disturbed or agitated state," (Merriam-Webster.com) and "a disturbance of the normal condition of the atmosphere" (Dictionary.com). Wow! Can you relate to that?

Many times, during my storms, I wanted nothing more than to skip the pain — physical or emotional — that I was feeling and hurry up the process, so I could get to the other side where it was done and the pain was gone. Does that sound familiar? I later found out through my therapy sessions that this was the exact thing I shouldn't be doing, but rather what I actually needed to go through. I had to feel the pain in order to heal properly from it. I needed so desperately to have someone tell me when I woke up the following morning, that the pain I was feeling would somehow disappear and my life would be peaceful again. This, not surprisingly, never occurred. But what did happen was that I made it through my storms, found the strength to own them, learn and grow from them, and know they had not defeated me. The empowerment that comes from this awareness is priceless and something I wish and pray for everyone to experience.

Let's be honest. There's something comforting about knowing that someone else has gone through and came out of what we're personally experiencing that gives us even a glimmer of hope. That is one of the reasons for this book. I promised God right in the middle of my storm that if it was what I needed to go through, He knew best, and I would take what I learned and help someone else. I did not want to waste the pain I was experiencing.

I may not know exactly what specific storm you're in right now, but I wish with everything within me that I could wrap my arms around you and tell you that it will be okay. I know there's a strong possibility you need that because I needed it. You may not even be the affectionate type, but there's something about a hug at the right time by the right person and being told it WILL be okay that makes us feel as though we will truly conquer the battle in front of us. Every single time someone would tell me that I would be okay, I held on to that statement with dear life because I wanted to truly believe it. That feeling of believing everything would be okay may have been short lived, but it did help me, even if for a moment. My prayer is that you can feel my heart in this book as a person who empathizes with you to the best of my God-given ability. And if you have not had anyone tell you yet, dear friend, or you just need to hear it again…you WILL make it through this storm.

Since I can't physically be there to hug you, I invite you to allow yourself to be embraced by Someone who can be there for you. Someone who wants to be there for you and Someone who genuinely cares about your well-being. No, you may not physically feel His presence (it is possible though), but I guarantee you with everything in my soul that He is there. Look for Him. Call out to Him. He will answer. Cry until you can't cry anymore. He will wipe your tears away. Feel the way you feel and do not feel ashamed about it. Open up to Him. He can handle it. He created you, so He already knows how you feel. I've done all the above and have honestly felt even just an ounce better. And feeling just an ounce better, my friend, is progress. God says in Jeremiah 33:3 (NIV), *"Call to me and I will answer you and tell you great and unsearchable things you do not know."*

There's not a lot in life I strongly hate. I'm not talking about a certain food or spiders. I'm talking about atrocious things such as racism, abuse of any sort, etc. There are, however, three words that I stand firmly in saying I will never be okay with — Get…over…it.

17

First, let me say that if you've ever told someone that, please know I'm not condemning you for it, as that is not my position nor place. God does not condemn us for our mistakes, but He does lovingly convict us. I pray you feel conviction if you ever spoke these words. That may sound harsh, but let me explain my position.

When you're in the middle of the storm, it feels like the worst thing ever…for you. Remember, what one person may consider a storm, another person may consider a cloudy day meaning they have a greater capacity to deal with the storm. For example, having a miscarriage for me, and many other women, was extremely devastating. After years of struggling with infertility, I simply could not fathom why this would happen. For someone else, it may not carry as much weight as it carried with me. And for someone who has never experienced a miscarriage but just hears about it, they may not truly understand why this loss brings so much devastation, especially in the early stages of pregnancy. There are a lot of different factors that come into play on how much you can handle a certain situation. We all are raised and socialized differently. A lot of these differences include social class, race, ethnicity, age, family structure, and religious background. This is not an exhaustive list, but certainly some of the main factors.

I've been on the receiving end of someone telling me that it was time for me to get over it. In the moment it occurred, I felt like my heart was literally about to explode. I was already feeling down because of circumstances that happened due to my divorce and I felt like I had a safe place in this person to share. We both mutually shared what we had been going through although both of our situations were very different. I knew the person meant me no harm, but to hear those words truly made me feel like I was back at square one in the healing process.

Your storm is YOUR storm and it's absolutely okay to feel how you feel in the middle of it. It is no one's job nor place to tell you how to grieve or how to move forward. Please notice what I just said. No one can tell you HOW to move forward. However, you do have to find your own way TO move forward. Even as I write this, I'm prayerful that my words are coming across as sensitive and as heartfelt as possible. I'm aware that you may be reading this and may have experienced a storm of life I have never experienced. I do not know what it feels like personally to lose a child...one of the worst and most tragic storms I could ever imagine going through. I don't know what it's like to lose a spouse to death. I do not know what's it like to be completely homeless and have nowhere to turn. I do know, however, that every person deserves the right to grieve the way they feel is necessary, no matter what they're going through.

I read so many books in my storm that I couldn't keep them all straight and at times I don't remember where I read what. I'm grateful though because I knew God was using every single one of those books, most importantly my Bible, to compassionately speak to me in my storm. I am forever grateful for the one devotional I read that told me that I was okay to feel what I was feeling. I desperately needed to hear that in that moment and I promised I would pass that message forward.

My dear friend, if you haven't had someone tell you yet, I want to be the first to tell you that you WILL make it through. Take your time; there is no rush. And while you're in the middle of your storm, call on the name of Jesus and know that He will be there to carry you every step of the way.

As I write this book, and even more specifically, as I write this chapter, I am smackdab in middle of my storm — rain, winds, clouds and, of course, hail and hell. It's starting to let up a bit, but it's still raining, the wind is slightly blowing, the clouds are a lighter shade of gray, and the "hell" that's dropping isn't as big as it was a week or so ago. In a matter of two weeks, I went from the highest of high feelings in learning I would be bringing a new life into the world to having a miscarriage, a D&C, a confrontation with my ex-husband, and surgery. Did I mention that during this timeframe I was in the middle of planning a surprise 80th birthday party for my beloved grandmother? Oh, and did I mention, I was wrapping up teaching a college semester, which brings being "on" for students who require your undivided attention, letters of recommendations, final grades, final exams, and lots of grading? My students see me as "Professor Campbell" who has a positive disposition and who has it all together, not as a broken woman who's gone through divorce, miscarriage, surgery, and bouts of depression all within the past two years and even in the midst of teaching. Oh, and did I mention I'm a single mom? (exhale!)

I have cried out to God so much over the past three years. Yet I can honestly say in the middle of that pain and the tears, I tried my best to stay as close to God as possible. He's brought me too far and I know Him to be real so my go-to is to turn to Him when I need to feel comfort. However, at a time where I needed Him the most, I didn't feel Him. I called out, I prayed, I cried not just a few tears, but the sort of cry that leaves you feeling like you're drowning in your own tears, and I asked Him the question we will *all* ask at some point in our life— Why?

I want to throw in a little note about asking the question "Why?" There is absolutely nothing wrong in this world about asking the question "Why?" That is a natural response we all have. I would challenge you, however, to ask "why?" instead of "why me?" I often hear people ask the latter —"why is (blank) happening to *me*?" When you ask in this way, you're basically, maybe not intentionally, saying, "Why is this happening to me INSTEAD of someone else?" You're basically saying one of two things. One, you're saying "this shouldn't be happening to me, but it should be happening to someone else." Second, you're essentially saying that something "bad" or "devastating" SHOULDN'T be happening to you, as in you are immune to calamities. Every single person on this God-given earth will experience trials. John 16:33 (NLT) states, *"I have told you all this so that you may have peace in me. Here on earth you will have many trials and sorrows. But take heart, because I have overcome the world."* Many times, we do or say things because it's always been said, or we heard other people say it, without giving much thought to what we are saying. There is power in words. They help to shape our thoughts, for better or for worse.

I wish I had started this book in the midst of going through all my different storms in life, although I can say, none proved to be as trying as what the last several years brought. I'm sure it would have been not only therapeutic for me, it would have given you better insight into the very real feelings I was experiencing and might, in some way, have helped you through your storm. I am left for much of this book to rely on my memory of how I was feeling in those exact moments, which may balance out the "right in the moment" experiences that I will openly share with you.

No one gets married if they really foresee themselves getting a divorce. I was truly one who absolutely never thought my sixteen-year marriage would end in divorce. I truly believed we were the exception. Call it ignorance, being naïve, having faith, or just plain hopeful, but that is where I was. There was absolutely no inward or outward sign, until the very end, that our family of three would be torn apart. No one could convince me that the day would come where our only child would have to go visit her dad at his apartment instead of waking up to both her parents under one roof. I would have never believed that the life we worked so diligently to build together and protect would soon only be a memory.

For fifteen years, the word divorce was never uttered once by either of us. *We* both knew that divorce would not be an option. I remember my ex-husband telling me one day as we stood in our kitchen that he had found everything he needed in a spouse in me. He probably doesn't remember, but when a wife is told something like that, she never forgets it. The reassurance that comes from that statement is very comforting. Yet, here I sit, as I write this book, divorced, my ex-husband now remarried to his former co-worker, and me at times, still trying to make sense of what happened. Divorce. Such a horrible word. A word I just knew would never be a part of my personal journey.

It's disastrous that so many families are affected by divorce. I understand that now more than ever since it has hit me personally with my own marriage. My parents were divorced, and all my grandparents were divorced. My brother was divorced and two of my ex-husband's five siblings were divorced. My ex-husband had even been married and divorced before. It hits you in a completely different way, however, when it's your very own relationship. To say it's like having the air knocked out of you is an understatement.

As a society, we hear about divorce so much, I believe, we unfortunately have become desensitized to it. I was definitely guilty of that. You sympathize to the best of your ability, but until you go through it personally, you are completely oblivious to just how much pain, confusion, depression, anger, and turmoil it brings. We've all been on the receiving end of hearing the news of "so and so's" divorce. While people hear you are divorced and may have a moment of saying, "Oh, wow! I'm so sorry!" with all sincerity, they soon move on in their day and you are left still reeling from the intense pain trying any and everything to make the pain subside.

My divorce, to date, is one of the greatest storms in my life, but the after effects of what it brought has simultaneously been a huge challenge in my life that has left me leaning on God more than I ever thought possible. It took me crying, praying, reading, researching, and finally uncovering that my entire marriage was spent with a narcissist. Coming into this revelation brought pain and peace all at the same time.

My ex-husband and I were able to get through most of our divorce amicably. We opted for a collaborative divorce in which we, as well as our lawyers, worked together in a sort of roundtable fashion to come to an agreement on everything from finances to custody. This kept us out of court. Even in the middle of this storm, I counted this as a blessing as I know so many people who couldn't stomach being in each other's presence in the midst of a divorce, so any amicable conversation was not even an option. Now anyone who knows anything about narcissism knows that this may not seem a characteristic of a narcissist. To be able to get through anything amicably is often not the case with someone who has this personality trait. However, one of the most impactful books that I have ever read, *The Human Magnet Syndrome*, illuminates how often there is a spectrum that people fall on from one to five. My ex-husband was definitely not a five, but given the characteristics he displayed in our marriage, prior and after the divorce, he would be unofficially classified at around a level three.

In the early months when we were first separated, there was no fighting between my ex-husband and I over our daughter. Even after my ex-husband moved out, he would still come by the house most evenings to see our daughter. I know God was heartbroken with our choice to divorce. However, even in going through it, God had His hand over me. God reminded me of James 1:1-4 often throughout my entire divorce process. I found hope in knowing that my trial and storm would not be wasted. I hated to go through it, but God was with me every step of the way building up my perseverance that would eventually serve a bigger purpose.

God spoke to me often throughout my storm. Sometimes it was through my Bible, other times it was through a book or devotional, and other times it was through a friend or my prayer partner. On one occasion in particular, my prayer partner told me that God would reveal to me the identity of the person my ex-husband was involved with. Leading up to our separation, my ex-husband revealed to me that someone else had his attention, however, he refused to disclose her identity to me. His explanation was that if I blew things out of proportion, things could end up really bad. I tried explaining to him that as his wife, I came first and, whatever this person had going on in their life, was NOT as important as his wife or our marriage or our family. Nothing I said to him seemed to get through to him.

All I knew was that he worked with this person. He could not understand how sick I felt watching him walk out the door every morning to go to work with this person he had feelings for while he was not giving me any assurance that he was not going to pursue this relationship.

This issue ultimately led to the end of our marriage. He decided to choose this person over his family and there was nothing I could do about it. To this day, he has never acknowledged that he chose her over my daughter and I, but he married her two years later and is with her to this day.

Although I had an idea who the person was, I had no way to prove it. Like any wife would, my imagination ran wild with wondering who the identity of this person was that my husband was so willing to protect. The lengths he was going to in order to keep her identity a secret confirmed so much more for me. He was willing to do all of this for this person, yet the tears I cried meant nothing after sixteen years of marriage. I had to conclude that my husband already had moved on emotionally. Learning that my ex-husband was a narcissist actually helped me to understand there was nothing I could have done to fix our marriage. It released the doubts I had about myself and helped to bring closure to all the questions that consumed me for the better part of three years. The cycle that a narcissist repeats in every relationship is to idealize, devalue, discard, and replace. Once I no longer could give him the narcissistic supply he needed, divorce was inevitable. He was already receiving his supply from his new source. Narcissists lack empathy. At times he was capable of this (remember, he is a level three, not a five), but it was short-lived. It now made sense why my tears made no difference to him. It now made sense why a man could so easily leave his second marriage to a woman he had one child with without looking behind to marry someone who just got out of an abusive relationship and who had been married twice, all the while playing dad to her children who each had dads of their own. This revelation brought about a level of healing that I could only thank God for. It made all the sense in the world now why he was on to marriage number three.

One day, through the mouth of my own child, in a very innocent and nonchalant conversation, God revealed the identity of this woman. My daughter and I were driving after getting dinner and she mentioned seeing this person at the church she and her dad were attending. In that very moment, I knew. My ex-husband chose to be with a former employee of his with whom he had a ten-year plus working relationship at the same company.

I knew this woman. She worked directly for him. We were acquaintances more so than friends. I had spoken to her on several occasions at their job and had even met her oldest son a few times at their job.

A year or so prior to our divorce, my ex and I had gone out with her and her now ex-husband (and some of their other co-workers) on a few occasions. Her and her husband had sat right across from us at the dinner table as we all spoke, laughed, and ate. And finally, the Valentine's Day prior to our separation, which occurred in March of 2016, my ex surprised me with dinner out to a nice restaurant and secretly arranged for babysitting for my daughter. Can you guess who the babysitter was? We went to her house to pick up my daughter, so I had been inside this woman's house. And to add to the already theatrics to this story, her ex-husband used to work at the same company that she and my ex-husband worked. The emotional storm was in full effect!

A few years later I wish I could say that my ex and I have remained amicable. There were a few moments here and there, but that came to a quick end. Through my research on narcissism, I learned that no contact is the best route to take when dealing with someone with this mental condition. They have their own reality that is often skewed and trying to co-parent effectively is near impossible.

The goal of explaining my divorce is to help others by sharing my personal experience as factually as I can and to let you know you're not alone in going through a storm. Divorce changes you. It can change you in a positive or negative way. It all depends on which way you deliberately and intentionally decide to go. I'm not saying that going through a divorce is a positive experience; it is not.

Even in relationships where a divorce is absolutely necessary due to abuse, going through the divorce is definitely not a pleasant experience.

One of the sociology courses I teach is on the subject matter of families. In all of my classes, I allow for ample class discussion and this class in particular always brings out relevant stories shared by several of my students. I have heard through the mouths of my students directly that even though they may have had a bad marriage or experienced their parents' tumultuous relationships that needed to end in divorce, the divorce was no less painful.

After a divorce, the life you've known and grown comfortable and accustomed to is now over. Whenever I have described my divorce, I always explained to anyone who was surprised by this outcome that we went from zero to one-hundred very quickly. What I meant by this was that we didn't have a turbulent marriage. One of the things we were both guilty of, however, was being overly non-confrontational, which some think is not a bad thing at all. The problem is when both people are this way, many issues are swept under the rug and not dealt with. No relationship is without confrontation. It's how you deal with that confrontation that matters. We both failed in this area. Like a good friend told me: when you sweep things under the rug, all you're doing is making the pile bigger until one day the rug can't hold all that dirt anymore. In a way, that is a lesson and blessing I learned in my storm.

Reigning in the Storm

There were countless times during this storm where I experienced several wonderful blessings from God. It was an indescribable feeling of going through the worse pain you have ever felt while simultaneously hearing from and feeling God's presence. I've always known God to be real, but because of my own sins and selfishness, I have at times felt very distant from him.

Often, we're conditioned to see only the negative when going through the storm. We feel the intense winds, see the rain, the "hell," and the storm clouds. Sometimes it can be weeks before we see the sun shine. It's important to remember that there is always something positive in a storm. Always. I will address blessings in the storm in another chapter.

When going through your storm, you may feel waking up every day is a punishment. The storm of your life may have you feeling as though you simply want to be left alone and not interact with anyone at all. I've been there. But it's important to remember that there are many people who wished they had an ounce of your energy to get out of bed. And the fact that you're getting out of bed is a blessing! I remember telling myself and learning to be okay with taking every day one hour at time. Taking everything one day at a time simply felt like a monstrous task I couldn't complete. Hour by hour was all I could do at times. But praise be to our God who will carry us through in as small of increments as we need.

God WILL take care of you if you allow Him to. Stop right here and reread that last sentence. It's so very important to me that you understand that and feel that. God WILL take care of you if you allow Him to.

Chapter 2

And the Storm Continues....

Consider it pure joy, my brother and sisters, whenever you face trials of many kinds because you know that the testing of your faith produces perseverance; let perseverance finish its work so that you may be mature and complete, not lacking anything. —James 1:1-4 (NIV)

As I work on parts of this particular chapter in April 2018, I sit in one of my favorite restaurants after leaving work early. I sit here eating, working, and doing everything to keep from going home to sit in the quiet of my house so my mind won't focus on those three dreadful words I heard on the other end of the phone line —" It's a miscarriage." I received that phone call at about 6 p.m. the previous evening while watching my 12-year-old daughter play in her softball game and surrounded by many other spectators. I kept my voice low and an eye on the game as I responded to the nurse about what was to come in the next few days and told her I would wait for her call the next day with more details. I not only wanted to cry, I absolutely needed to. I needed to scream, yell, and cry, all at the same time. But in the midst of my daughter's game and sitting there alone, I kept my composure, at least until I got home.

A miscarriage is devastating — period. I won't dare say one person's experience is worse when compared to the next. All I can do is share why my particular situation was extremely difficult for me.

Through this past year, I've grown so close to God that, while keeping my reverence and respect for Him, I simultaneously learned to be completely open and honest with Him. I've learned to get past the "formal" type prayer, which at times serves a purpose, and have learned to just talk to Him like the friend and Father He is. And boy, had He heard it the past forty-eight hours leading up to this moment of writing!

Let me begin with my background story when it comes to having children. My ex-husband and I tried pretty much our entire sixteen years of being married to have children. I went through surgery and two failed rounds of in-vitro fertilization, which is an emotional rollercoaster in itself. We were extremely blessed to eventually get pregnant miraculously and naturally with our beautiful daughter, Jadyn. Infertility issues can take a toll on any couple. We pushed past it, but in the end, I'm sure the years of disappointment left a hole in the both of us.

Second Corinthians 12 tells the story of the thorn in Paul's side. Many of us are familiar with what Jesus reminds us in the 9th verse, *"My grace is sufficient for you for my power is made perfect in your weakness"* (NIV). Infertility has been the thorn in *my* side. We all have one or two or three, but not being able to have more children when I strongly desired them was mine. For you, it may be repeated bad relationships, insecurity, finances, drugs, alcohol, stress, or illnesses. The list goes on and on and on.

There was a period of my life where there was always a corner of bitterness in my heart whenever I heard of someone else having a child. I could smile and congratulate whenever necessary, but I often struggled with God in that I had this strong desire to be a mom, but I couldn't naturally fulfill it. I heard stories of parents who abused or neglected kids or choose to not be a part of their lives and wondered if they have an inkling at how special children are and that there are those of us who would do anything to be blessed with another. If you or someone you know has battled this same storm, you know exactly what I am saying. So, needless to say, another storm of mine was the storm of infertility.

Fast forward some years through the storm of getting divorced after sixteen years of marriage, and I now have a wonderful boyfriend who is absolutely my best friend. Then one morning, we get the surprise of probably both of our lives — a positive pregnancy test! (three tests to be exact! Had to be *sure*!) No, definitely not exactly what we planned, but obviously "it was meant to be" or at least that's what we and everyone else felt and kept saying. After two days of initial shock, the excitement settled in for us both, and for me, in particular, there was not a single part of me that was not excited about this new bundle I was about to hold in my arms in nine months.

Now let me stop hear and address something important. I'm very much aware that someone may read this book and find it a bit contradictory that I talk about my love for God, my faith, and being a Christian, yet end up pregnant and not married. And to add to that please remember, I'm also divorced. I get and sometimes stay angry and find it hard to forgive certain people, and the list of sins that I have go on. I would ask you to stop and remember a few things.

My relationship with Christ comes before everything else. I define myself unequivocally as a Christian and will be until the day I take my last breath. I do my best every day to treat others the way I believe Christ would want me to and I truly enjoy that. Most days, it does come effortlessly for me. However, I'm also human...a flawed human. I've sinned. I've acted in my anger, I've had moments where I've stopped trusting God, I question God, and the list goes on. Truthfully, I probably sin daily. But I praise God for sending His Son to die for my sins. I thank God for forgiving me daily and renewing me with grace and mercy each morning I wake up. I'm not condoning my pregnancy that occurred while not being married, but I also don't view it negatively. This book has come about because of and in spite of my sins. Ephesians 1:7 (NIV) reminds us, *In Him we have redemption through His blood, the forgiveness of sins, in accordance with the riches of God's grace.* Hallelujah! If my problems, issues, sins, and storms are what it takes to help in encouraging another person, my friend, it is all worth it.

Back to my pregnancy. I wanted to tell everyone, as I'm sure every expectant mom does, but we tried our best to keep it contained to close family and friends. Every single person was excited! Everyone saw the blessing in this, especially my family who knew of my past infertility struggles. And then there was one of the most exciting parts — my daughter was finally going to be a big sister, and boy, was she the perfect age. They would be a weird twelve or thirteen years apart since Jadyn's birthday started the year in January, but the baby was due in December.

Everything with this pregnancy lined up perfectly! The timing of my job — I was finishing up a semester teaching so I could be home with my morning sickness for the remainder of my first trimester. And we had a trip planned home to California at the start of my second trimester (bye-bye morning sickness!), and my due date was literally three days after the end of the fall semester. I couldn't have planned it any better myself if I had tried!

My mom and I were amused at the fact I was the exact same age she was when she had my baby sister, who came eighteen years after me! As for my boyfriend, who was in a situation where he was not seeing his kids because they were with his ex-wife, he looked at it as the blessing of being given another chance to freely be in his child's life. I completely felt like I heard from God through scripture and books I was reading. It's the furthest thing from my nature to blame something on God if I wholeheartedly do not believe it was from Him. In fact, sometimes He has to convince me twice. Everything with this pregnancy just made sense!

So, hearing those three words, or maybe I should say hearing the confirmation, felt like the worst pain in the world. Why would God reopen a wound that I had diligently patched up? Here I was, thirty-seven years old, a year divorced and being very intentional about my healing. I was starting my own business in addition to working a job I absolutely loved, staying busy with my daughter and her activities, happily in another relationship. I was joyfully moving forward with my life. Then out of nowhere, what occurred was what I referred to as an unnecessary storm. (I've come to realize that no storm is unnecessary, but that is truly how I felt in that moment.)

We may not always understand the "why" of a storm, but there's a purpose for or a lesson to be learned in EVERY storm, you just have to look for it. To this day, I still don't understand the "why," but had I not gone through it, it wouldn't be a part of my book to maybe help someone else. That's a blessing in itself.

If you focus on the deafening sounds of the storm's booms, or the thunder strikes that can catch a house on fire, or the pouring rain that can cause flooding, you will miss the beautiful lit up sky and the nourishment our plants and grass receive from the pouring rain that will make them grow taller, stronger, and healthier.

When my daughter was little she would ask to go out and play in the rain —and I was completely okay with saying yes! Why? Because I wanted her to realize that we shouldn't go run and hide every time there's a little rain outside. Plus, we live in south Texas where, even when it's pouring, it can be warm outside. But just like the time she came running into the house when the booms of thunder got too loud, we are privileged that we can go running into our Father's house or arms when life feels too overwhelming.

I'm known for saying and loving the quote, "if it were easy everyone would do it." I'm very much a realist in many ways so I stand here and say unequivocally it is not easy making it to the other side of the storm. In fact, I know firsthand sometimes it feels near impossible. Just like a storm often knocks out the power supply in your home, a life storm will knock out the energy in your physical home — your body. You feel hopeless, depressed, angry, sad, scared, and anxious — often all at the same time. A storm not only knocks you out emotionally, it can knock out your physical energy as well.

It felt like the hardest thing in the world, at the time, to get in front of my sociology class on families and maintain my professionalism while talking about all the good, bad, and ugly of family life. All while I was right in the middle of my own family crisis of divorce. It felt completely unfair. I stood in the middle of my health class where I lectured on the high infant mortality rates of African Americans while I was five weeks pregnant, only to leave class early after feeling sick to find out later I was sick because I was having a miscarriage right there at work. I felt like I was drowning all the mornings I woke up and wiped the tears from the daughter's eyes and told her things would be okay after me and her dad had divorced, only to wait until I dropped her off at school on my way to work and have to wipe my own tears.

I share this not for sympathy, but to let you know, I'm still standing. Not only am I standing, I'm smiling. I'm standing and smiling while being stronger. I can honestly say I'm reigning in my storm, just as you will reign in yours.

Chapter 3

Lost in the Storm

If it were an enemy insulting me, I could bear it. If it were my enemies attacking me, I could hide
But it is you, the one so close to me, my companion, my good friend, who does this" – Psalms 55:12-13 (ERV)

Very few people I know enjoy the feelings that come with being lost. There are always the outliers in life who love the adventure and endless possibilities that come from being lost, but that's truly not me. Anxiety creeps in, uncertainty, and often times frustration. When we find ourselves in a situation where we feel lost, the very first thing we want to do is find our way back to the main path. Typically, we look for signs, signals, or we even try to retrace our steps so that we can get back to a place of familiarity.

I couldn't imagine being truly lost in one of nature's storms. The sight of knocked-down, broken trees, wind blowing, power lines down, water everywhere, and darkness is the illustration that pops up in my head when I think of a catastrophic storm. I imagine crying out for help to any person who may hear so that I can get back to a place of safety. There are many situations in life that can leave us feeling lost: divorce, death, bankruptcy, infertility or miscarriages, natural disasters, broken relationships, and more. Many times, the pain that is inflicted upon us from our closest relationships leave us feeling like we do not know which way to turn.

How do you deal with betrayal? And I don't mean that as a passive, rhetorical type question. I seriously want to know how YOU deal with betrayal? Think about that situation of betrayal for just a second. If you've ever been betrayed, you know firsthand that the feelings and thoughts you experienced or are currently experiencing are such that…well…let's just say they wouldn't put you at the front of the line in heaven! Let me share how I dealt with it and maybe you can relate to some of my feelings.

Disgust. Sadness. Extreme anger. Confusion. These are some of the feelings I experienced deep within my most inner being in November of 2018 as I continued on in my storm. How do you look at the person who was once your companion, protector, and spouse for almost twenty years, the person who was supposed to be by your side until the very end, knowing that they are intentionally trying to hurt you? That, by far, is one of the worst feelings I experienced in my storm and, truthfully, in my life. Let me explain.

When my ex-husband and I decided to divorce, we agreed that if there eventually was another person involved in our lives romantically who would be around our daughter, we would give the other parent the courtesy to meet that person. Seems pretty reasonable and simple, right? Well, due to the fact that my ex-husband had started a relationship with his girlfriend prior to our marriage ending, and due to the fact that I "knew" her because of their work relationship as coworkers and then him as her boss, he was not so quick to respond to my requests for she and I having a sit-down conversation regarding Jadyn.

During the summer of 2018, my ex-husband sent me an email, which was pretty much the best way for us to correspond with one another, about us working out sharing our daughter for Thanksgiving. As he did the previous year, which was our first Thanksgiving post-divorce, he wanted to take our daughter to Disneyland. (He literally and figuratively was the living and breathing perfect example of a true "Disneyland dad.") We came to the agreement that he would have her the few days leading up to Thanksgiving and he would have her back to me on Thanksgiving morning. For the first half of our divorce, we were able to pretty much manage without the custody agreement and work things out to the best of our ability regarding our daughter. He traveled a lot with his job, so she pretty much lived with me and would visit him sporadically when he was home. He would email me ahead of time and, more times than not, if we had nothing planned, I agreed she could spend several days with him. For the most part, it worked out well and kept a sense of stability to her life. We agreed to do what was best for her and keep things as amicable as we possibly could for her sake — our one and only daughter. Up until this point, we had kept the courts out of everything, but this soon changed.

Around the first week of November, Jadyn informed me that it wasn't just she and her dad traveling over 1,000 miles away to California, but it was she, her dad, his girlfriend, and her two sons — details that he conveniently left out of our original conversation. I've already given the backstory on the girlfriend, now wife, but what I haven't mentioned is that for the better part of a year and a half, I requested to have a sit-down conversation, mother to mother, with this other woman who was now in my daughter's life. I had upheld my end of the bargain with him speaking to my boyfriend, yet he had not reciprocated.

Given that this request of mine was not granted, I did not feel comfortable sending Jadyn so far away with someone who was choosing not to speak with me, woman to woman, but more importantly mother to mother, so I informed Jadyn and her dad that until that conversation happened, I was not in agreement of her going on this trip. As a mom, I had very specific questions I needed and wanted answered from the other adult who would be responsible for Jadyn if something should happen to her dad. To not have this conversation with me, despite my negative feelings towards her, was very irresponsible, on her part, in my opinion.

Due to my mandate of a conversation with his girlfriend, my ex became quite upset (narcissism in full swing!) and decided to bring a sheriff to my house to get our daughter within a matter of two hours of me telling him. This was not for the best interest of our daughter. He did it simply because he

was being spiteful towards me and because I had
challenged him. Involving law enforcement over
something so trivial and something that could be
remedied on our own went against everything we
strived to do for our daughter. It became very
apparent to me that our daughter's best interest was
not a priority for him. He was doing this simply for
him. Of course, from a narcissist's point of view, the
damage was all being caused by me.

My daughter immediately broke down crying
wanting to know if the sheriff was going to make her
go. I explained to her that I honestly did not know,
but we would have to wait and see. The sheriff and
her dad showed up to my house and I spoke with the
sheriff explaining the Disneyland trip situation to
him. He fully agreed with my decision in not
sending Jadyn on a plane with someone who
wouldn't talk to me and he made my ex-husband
leave. This was the beginning of what has
unfortunately become a strained relationship
between Jadyn and her father.

The next week involved us both speaking with
our lawyers. I was attempting to set up a sit-down
with his girlfriend with a mediator, which I agreed to
pay for, but my ex would not agree to it without
being present. Things were going from bad to worse
very quickly. All went quiet for a few days, but my
gut told me something was up; I just didn't know
what. Well, my gut was right. My ex had me served
with papers at our daughter's theater rehearsal at
10:00 at night to appear in court in less than forty-
eight hours to get the judge to sign off on her going

on their trip, instead of agreeing to let his girlfriend and I speak. (Crazy I know!) I had one day to find an attorney, pay lawyer's fees I had not planned on spending, take a day off of work, and get ready to go to court. (And did I mention this was all so his girlfriend and I wouldn't sit down and have a conversation without him present? *And* did I mention this was all for Disneyland?) By this point, Jadyn really didn't care if she went one way or not. She just wanted all of this to be over, as did I.

Well, one downhome, old school lesson I have learned in life that is so true is this… "God don't like ugly!" Not only did I find and secure an amazing lawyer, she really went to bat for me. The end result was the judge ordering his girlfriend to sit down that evening and talk with me prior to their trip, which was the next day. It was such a ridiculous and unnecessary experience! As angry and frustrated as I was that I had to spend $2500 unexpectantly on this issue that could have been resolved the week prior for only $130 for a mediator to be present, or better yet for *free*, I knew God showed up on my behalf because of my faithfulness to Him. Second Thessalonians 3:3 states, *"But the Lord is faithful; He will strengthen you and guard you from the evil one."* Amen and hallelujah!

I can sleep well at night and have confidence in putting this truth in this book — I have never spoke negatively about my ex to our daughter. (Please don't make the mistake in thinking I didn't want to though! Lord knows I wanted to! Just being honest!) I have done everything to be intentional about my healing and hers, and truthfully, everything I do is for her. It was not easy at times, but I had to train myself to look past the current moment of temporary satisfaction that I may or may not receive in speaking ill of him and to look ahead knowing that temporary satisfaction would equate to a long-lasting negative impact on her life. The trade-off was not worth it and I'm grateful to God who helped me to understand that. If I speak negatively of her father, I have learned and understood that will have a lasting adverse effect on her, even into her adulthood. I'm sure my ex takes the stance that he's doing every and anything for our daughter as well. Here lies the difference though. Through the toughest and most challenging storm of my life, I committed myself to being more Christlike and I allowed God to take control completely of every situation I faced. Does that mean I didn't mess up and say something out of anger to him or try to grab the wheel out of God's hand and do it myself because I felt like He was moving too slow? Of course not. I'm human. I'm flawed. I have several imperfections! But, even more than that, I own my position as a child of God who is forgiven and shown grace and mercy. If you put God first, He will show up for you *everytime*!

The feeling of being attacked and made out to be something else from someone you shared seventeen years of life with, is not only the worst feeling, it's treachery at the highest level in my book. Psalms 55:12-14 speaks of David's feeling of being betrayed by a companion. This is worse than being betrayed by an enemy because that enemy is doing what you would expect them to do. The feeling of betrayal by a companion is one that damages your innermost soul. As I sit and write this and know that I'm closer to God than at any time ever in my life, I must continue to pray and ask God to help me move forward and allow Him to take away the pain and replace it with healing and forgiveness. I share that with you so that you know and understand I'm human; we're all human. No one has this Christ walk down pat. And if you think someone does and never admits any flaws to you, run the other way!

By now, I've had my fair share of being in the eye of the storm. I'm not a quitter by any stretch of the imagination. When I put my mind to something, it usually gets done. But at this moment in my storm, I literally feel like quitting. I feel like throwing my hands up and saying, "I'm done!" I'm not exactly sure what I want to be done with, but that's just the feeling I'm experiencing. I am tired of stressing, I am tired of crying, and I am tired of being tired. Have you ever felt that way? I experienced this wanting to give up feeling all while still having to go to work to teach and take on the duties of a being a single mom. I'm truly not a complainer, but I was ready to just be done with it all. Jadyn was stressed, I was stressed, and we both really just wanted to get on with our lives. My ex just wanted his cake and to be able to eat it too. He wanted his new family and wanted everything to turn out perfectly with Jadyn when, in reality, we were both hurting in our own ways. In many ways, she and I both were still trying to make sense of what happened to the security of our family.

We simply wanted to establish our new normal and just get through each day without any pain.

As I mentioned in the previous chapter, I learned that it is near impossible to co-parent effectively with a narcissist. You (the ex of the narcissist) are no longer valuable as a supply and literally become the enemy and kids are often not put first. Because narcissists are mainly focused on themselves, if something or someone does not benefit them anymore, they or that thing is of no use to them anymore. I didn't realize any of this at the beginning of our divorce or even during our marriage, but knowledge is truly powerful and knowing and understanding this came as double-edged sword.

I wanted Jadyn to have a relationship with her father for no other reason than I understood the importance of it for a daughter. My ex had painted me, however, in a light where he was the victim and I was intentionally trying to keep our daughter away from him. I was able to compartmentalize and keep marital issues separate from parenting issues. I will admit this can be extremely hard to do at moments when you allow your emotions to get the best of you. However, the other edge of the sword was that his narcissistic attitude and behaviors were truly adding stress to both our daughter and I, and he simply chose not to see that. He viewed life through a completely different lens. How do you find a balance of making sure your daughter has a relationship with her father yet also keep her emotionally safe from his emotional toxicity? Narcissists do not believe they are narcissists. They chalk that up to something being wrong with you and blaming you for everything, so you literally are left with the ultimate decision of handling the narcissist in the way they must be dealt with — no contact. In a case where you share kids, no contact should be as minimal of contact as possible.

On a cool December morning, as I walked up my walkway after getting home from dropping off Jadyn at school, I heard this one very clear and distinct word from God — reset. The definition of reset is "to set, adjust, or fix in a new or different way." That is exactly what I heard God tell me to do. I simply didn't know what He meant by this.

For the past six weeks, life for both Jadyn and I had become extremely difficult, stressful, and flat out exhausting. I was seeing my twelve-year old pull away from activities she once loved, wake up sad more mornings than not, and I was feeling like I was barely keeping it together myself. Our stability had been shaken at the hands of this ugly divorce and custody situation. At the same time, my relationship with my boyfriend was becoming more and more stressful with more frequent arguments, which added additional stress. At a time and place when I needed to feel safe emotionally, I didn't, and my peace was slowly sliding away.

For the better part of a year and half, Jadyn lived with me full-time. The first year of our divorce, my ex-husband traveled a lot due to his job, so it simply made sense for her to live with me. She had no barriers as to when she could see her dad, but our lives did not stop to accommodate him. If we had no plans, activities, or engagements, she was welcome to spend as much time with her dad as she wanted. All of a sudden, he decided, out of anger towards me, that this was not working for him anymore.

Because of my request to talk to his girlfriend, he was now trying to make Jadyn go back and forth week-to-week from one home to another, without considering her feelings. He even attempted to "compromise" and came up with a schedule that went something like this: Monday at Mom's, Tuesdays-Thursday at Dad's, Friday-Sunday at Mom's, Monday at Mom's, Tuesday and Wednesday at Dad's, and so on. This would make even the sanest person crazy! In his narcissistic mind, this was what was best for him. For anyone who has not been through divorce and dealt with custody issues, let me be the first to say, aside from money, there isn't a more contentious issue. After all, both parents love their children equally and don't want to give up time spent with their child. Realistically, a 50/50 split is almost impossible to achieve. After Jadyn having a very set routine and stability for the past few years, my ex was dead set on coming up with his own rules. I say this again because it's so significant. This demand stemmed from anger towards me, not out of care for our daughter. This is what I meant by our stability was shaken. The uncertainty with her dad's demands was causing unnecessary stress to us both.

I walked into my house and sat down to pray and asked God to clarify what He meant by telling me I needed to reset. I felt as though He was telling me I needed to just stop and reset everything in my life, but how do I go about doing this? I thrive on structure, stability, harmony, and minimal chaos. However, every direction I turned there was instability and lots of chaos. I needed, mostly for Jadyn's sake, to reset everything. So, I did or at least I attempted to.

That same day I typed an email to my ex asking him to join me in resetting things for our one and only daughter. I explained how stressed she was and that some things needed to change. I remained as amicable as I could and felt that we may, for once, finally agree on this for the sake of our daughter, despite the ugliness of the past month. His response was for the three of us to meet after she got out of school that day, so we could come up with a solution on how to move forward.

I wish I could say that our meeting together went well, and we were able to compromise but remember, I was dealing with a narcissist who was looking out for himself. It broke my heart to witness what our daughter so often told me about her dad — that he just wouldn't *listen* to her. I watched as she attempted to explain to her dad, as lovingly as possible, that she just wanted things to go back to the way they were, but he would not budge. Ultimately, he backed her into a corner forcing her to choose between me and him. She chose to stay put with me, not because she loves her dad any less, but because he backed her into a corner and put a responsibility on her that should have never been placed on her.

I know people have gone through custody issues much more challenging than mine and my heart literally aches. Yes, for the parents, but more for the children. I'm a huge advocate of children being heard when they're in pain. Divorce brings about so many emotions that even the strongest of adults have a hard time processing them. Why do we place so much pressure on children to navigate these storms when often they're ill-equipped? Parents have to do better. We have to be the grown-ups that God requires us to be. Ephesians 6:4 (ERV) reads, *"Fathers, don't make your children angry, but raise them with the kind of teaching and training you learn from the Lord."*

Often times after a storm, buildings and any other structures that endured damage need to be reinforced with material more suitable to sustain the next storm; that way the next storm won't cause as much damage. It's unfortunate that so many structures are damaged in a storm and this is sometimes due to not being structurally sound and prepared. Reinforcements are put in place after a severe storm so the next storm that comes will not cause nearly as much damage as the first. This comes from being prepared.

Storms are inevitable. They WILL strike. Every storm is going to be individual. No matter what your storm, how you handle each one is going to better prepare you for the following storm. My prayer is that during and after each storm, you will place reinforcements in your life so that you're better prepared to handle whatever comes your way.

Modern technology has been a blessing in that our forecasters can typically predict the whereabouts and patterns of tropical storms that will turn into hurricanes, and their projected landfall dates. Sometimes the storm takes an unpredicted turn or sometimes it speeds up and makes landfall sooner than excepted. We're fortunate to have forecasters guide us through. However, the ultimate Forecaster in our lives should not be TV reporters, but it should be our Heavenly Father who sits on the throne and wants nothing more for us than to lean on Him during the storms of life.

The point in me sharing this story with you is to give you a glimpse inside the storm that caused me to feel like I was completing lost in my walk with God. Well, let me correct that. I didn't feel completely lost because by this point, God had shown Himself to me through much of the adversity I was facing. But it seemed like every corner I turned led me to a dead end when I was intentionally trying to heal. I'd back up, regain my composure, run a little further, and hit another dead end. I felt like the mouse trying to escape the maze it was placed in while someone, God, watched from above, waiting for me to find the exit. This analogy is only half accurate. I was running and feeling like I was lost, but in actuality I wasn't really lost. God was running alongside of me the entire time. The next time you feel lost in your storm, remember what God says in Isaiah 43:2-3 (MSG),*"When you're in over your head, I'll be there with you. When you're in rough waters, you will not drown. When you're between a rock and a hard place, it won't be a dead end — because I am God, your personal God."*

Reigning in the Storm

Chapter 4

Traveling Through Your Storm

But those who hope in the Lord will renew their strength. They will soar on wings like eagles; they will run and not grow weary, they will walk and not be faint.
—Isaiah 40:31 (NIV)

I mentioned before just how much I gravitated towards books, especially in the middle of a storm. In fact, one of the reasons I wrote this book was because I knew the power of another's positive words and the encouragement that you can receive, even on your darkest of days.

I truly have a lot of admiration and respect for the renowned Bible teacher and author, Joyce Meyer. Her teachings have truly helped me in my relationship with Christ and her no- nonsense approach was always heard just at the right time. In the previous four years or so leading up to writing this book, I had probably read about fifteen or so of her books; this does not include the devotionals I received through emails or on my Bible app. During the process of completing this book, there was one particular day I had listened to one of her programs in the morning on TV while I was getting ready for work. I selfishly believed what she said was meant just for me as I was in the middle of writing this book so thank you Joyce, for my message!

Prior to my divorce, prior to my miscarriage, and prior to my surgery, my life, although not without the occasional bumps and bruises, was pretty simple and "drama free." At least that's how I objectively viewed it. I say objectively because no life is without its rough patches, but I knew what my life looked like from the outside looking in. I didn't have a lot to complain about and even though the bumps did occur, I still had a partner who I felt I could lean on. Life always seems a bit less scary and more easily manageable when you know you have someone else there, even if that relationship isn't the best. There's comfort in the presence of another person. Innately, we crave companionship. Fast forward a few years and I can no longer say life is pretty simple.

Joyce made it very clear, as she often does. Essentially, she said that if you have *any* intention of helping anyone in life, you *will* go through some storms. Not only will you go through them, but you *have* to go through them. She ultimately stressed be careful about asking God to use you because not only will He use you, you will also have to travel some uncomfortable roads in order to get to where you're headed. Easy? Absolutely not! Worth it? Absolutely!

Storms are inevitable, so knowing how to navigate them will aid in the pain and the desperation you will feel in wanting to get through it as fast as possible. Like many, I can be pretty impatient and downright hard-headed about certain things in life.

This has usually played out for me during the numerous times in my life when I had to have surgery. Typically, after surgery, your doctor will give you instructions on how long you need to rest before starting back to your normal routine. I'm a busybody by nature so having to sit still is darn near impossible for me. Even if I'm sitting on my couch watching TV, I still have a need to be doing something else even if it's reading, working, writing my book, or looking up stuff online (I'm working on this problem)! It was a process for me, but I have grown in this area and have really worked at enjoying my "down" time because it rarely happens but is often needed.

My last surgery ironically happened in the middle of writing this book (a myomectomy to have fibroids removed for the second time in about six years). I was instructed to not "do this" for this period of time and not "do that" for that period of time. If you can imagine a five- year old pouting with their bottom lip all the way down to the ground, that was me after hearing this news. All I wanted to know was what was the very earliest, and I meant *earliest*, I could get back to my gym workouts!

These doctor's orders were in place for a reason. If I had started back to my workout regime too soon, I ultimately ran the risk of one of my incisions reopening and not healing properly. If this were to occur, my two weeks off would inevitably turn into four weeks off, which for this busybody would be the worst news ever. The point is, sometimes in life, we need to go through the challenges and if we try to rush the process, then we could ultimately put ourselves at risk of not healing properly or worst, making a bad situation worse.

One day while I was in a counseling session, I told my counselor I was sick and tired of feeling the way I felt. I was tired of crying. I was tired of hurting. I wanted it to hurry up and be over. I learned a very important lesson that day from her. If I had any desire to heal the proper way, I had to feel what I was feeling. I needed to sit with every hurt, ache, and wound I was experiencing. Is it uncomfortable? YES! As a matter of fact, it can be downright miserable. But you know what? She was right. I stopped trying to rush the process and I learned to sit in my feelings for a while. I learned to understand and accept that feeling the pain was part of the healing process. I heard it said that healing is not for the weak. You must be intentional. You must go through the storm in order to get to the other side.

So now that we understand that life will bring storms our way and that we must go through them, we now can be receptive to learning how to actually travel through a storm. On the surface, cars, airplanes, and eagles are all obviously different and they all handle storms very differently. Even as you read this, there's a good chance that you or someone you care about is surrounded by a storm. You may be waiting out your storm like a car, going head first into and through your storm like an airplane, or flying high above your storm like an eagle. Let's take a look at what I mean by all three of these.

Favor Campbell

When I was twenty years old, my ex-husband and I made a four-day journey in our car to move from California to Maryland. Somewhere around Ohio, we ran into some serious rainstorms like we had never experienced before. The rain was coming down so hard, we, as well as other motorists, pulled over to the side of the road to wait the storm out. Driving any further in this storm that we were so unfamiliar with could have been dangerous and could have ultimately lead to an accident. Sometimes in life, we need to just stop, and wait the storm out.

Waiting, however, doesn't necessarily mean you do nothing and let life pass you by. Waiting it out may mean putting aside the worry, the anxiety, the anger, the frustrations, and saying, "God, I'm waiting to hear from you on what to do next." During that time when we were traveling in the early 2000s, cell phones weren't what they are now. Had they been, our time "waiting" I'm sure would have consisted of checking the news on our phone or looking on a weather app to get an idea of how long we needed to wait or what we should do in the process. Doing these things may have given us some direction on which route to take, but leaving too soon could have been detrimental to our travel plans. Waiting it out can include preparing for the next step. Let me give you a practical example to put this into perspective.

About a year or so ago from writing this, my boyfriend absolutely hated the job he had. And when I say he hated it, he HATED it! He had his moments where he was thankful he had a job, but if he had his choice and could swing it, he would quit in a heartbeat. In the midst of looking for a new job, he got called in for an interview, nailed the interview, and pretty much got offered the job, only to have the government go through a hiring freeze, which eventually led to that particular job not being needed anymore. My heart ached seeing him so disappointed. Talk about being at the five-yard line only to have the ball ripped out of your hand!

One of the things I admired very much about him was his work ethic. I honestly have never met someone who has as strong of a work ethic as this man. While working his 9-5 that he hated, he also worked two part-time jobs — one teaching once a week and one proctoring during his off times. From pretty much the beginning of our relationship, he was constantly looking for another job, working on and updating his resume, and networking with people. There wasn't one day that went by that he didn't talk about the new job he knew he would eventually get. It was a long year, but eventually he landed that same job he interviewed for, which was an all-around much better fit for him. His attitude, happiness, and his overall well-being improved dramatically.

He could have easily gone home every night and complained to anyone who would listen, turn on the TV, and sulk about his circumstances, but he waited. . . and waited. . . and waited. But while he waited, he kept himself relevant, worked on his resume, and ultimately, with God's perfect timing, landed a much better job. Sometimes all you can do is pull over and wait the storm out. But always remember while waiting, you prepare for the sun that will shine again.

The Bible is our source to go to that has all the guidance we need in order to know how to wait out the storms of life. Lamentations 3:24 (NIV) states, *"I say to myself, 'The Lord is my portion; therefore I will wait for him.'"*

Unlike a car, that often needs to wait a storm out, an airplane will often fly right through the storm. The goal often is to get above it, but many times a storm is on the flightpath and the only way to get to the required flying altitude is to fly right through it. That may be where you are right now. An entire flight will not be flown through a storm, but before a plane reaches its final altitude, it will have to fly through the storm. The storm will cause you to feel some of that unwelcome turbulence, but on the other side of that is a calm, peaceful sky.

I'm prone to motion sickness so turbulence is especially an unwelcomed experience for me. Not only am I fighting the fear of a shaky plane, I'm also battling the inescapable and dreadful feeling of nausea. It's a bumpy ride that I want nothing more than to get off of, but I know in the moments to come, everything will smooth out. I don't know what storm you're flying through at this very moment. It could be the death of a loved one, infertility, divorce, defiant children, a loss of a job, financial difficulties, an unexpected medical diagnosis, and the list of course goes on. Going through it often is necessary in order to get to the smooth and peaceful skies that bring about healing. My hope and prayer is that you know even through this turbulent time, God will safely fly you through it if you allow Him to. Once we are out of the turbulent weather, it's time to soar high above the storm.

Eagles are synonymous Biblically with how to deal with the storms of life. Isaiah 40:31 is one of most commonly quoted scriptures when it comes to "renewing your strength" and "soaring on wings like eagles." I love The Message version that reads, *"But those who wait upon God get fresh strength. They spread their wings and soar like eagles."*

Flying above the storm means you're not focused on the wind, rain, and dark clouds that brew below. Your attention is on the majestic sky that is in front of you. This doesn't mean that your storm magically disappears. It means that you now, even if temporarily, take your focus off of the storm brewing below. For me, in the middle of my storm, this meant focusing even more on my daughter, her well-being, and her activities. The months following my divorce when the pain was still there, I also decided to start training for my third fitness competition. I also continued to work on the details of my own business and move this idea of mine to a reality. You see, the storm was still raging, but for my mental and physical health I needed to find clearer paths. When you fly above the storm, you're living above your circumstances and problems. The problems are there, but you focus on moving forward.

Every storm is going to be different. There may be similarities that surface from time to time, but the amazing thing is that we can grow and always be better prepared than the time before. Each storm will need to be handled differently. Ask yourself where you are so you can adjust how you navigate through this storm. Is it something you need to wait out, fly through bold and strong, or fly above until the winds calm down a bit? No matter where you are, rest assured God is right there carrying you every step of the way.

Chapter 5

Rebuilding During Your Storm

And I will bring my people Israel back from exile. They will rebuild the ruined cities and live in them. They will plant vineyards and drink their wine; they will make gardens and eat their fruit." –
Amos 9:14 (NIV)

During the summers of 2017 and 2018, there were several thunderstorms in my city that left a few homes in my neighborhood the unfortunate targets of lightning strikes. One of the homes was on my direct route home so daily, my daughter and I witnessed what was left of the burnt frame and the charred remains. These were daily reminders of the devastation that comes with having to rebuild. For the first few months the house looked to be at its weakest state. I can only imagine the disarray the family was in having to relocate and start rebuilding their home from the ground up. Just the thought of the process seemed overwhelming to me.

A few months after the lightning strike, what remained of the house was completely demolished. All that remained was the concrete slab that once held up a beautiful one-story brick house. A few months later the rebuilding began and slowly, but surely, the house started to be put back together, piece-by-piece. The frame went back up, then the drywall, and lastly the outside bricks and stone. But a month or so before the house was complete, I noticed that the house was being rebuilt somewhat different than the original. The homeowners had chosen new bricks and a new color scheme, which gave it a fresher look. There were also some other small decorative changes that really enhanced the beauty of the home. The layout and the floorplan of the house looked exactly the same, but I'm sure the inside of the home had been remodeled to match the new look on the outside. The house had been rebuilt and looked stronger and more beautiful than ever.

Rebuilding a house, in a lot of ways may be easier than the process of rebuilding yourself and your own life. In many ways, life for me was very stable up until literally the month my ex-husband moved out of our house. For ten years, I had been a stay-at-home mom, I had structure and stability, I had another person to go through life with then, all of sudden, the lightning struck. Hard. I had to quickly find a way to rebuild. I had only been working for two months and now I was a full-time working single mom. I had to figure out how to navigate life as a single woman in a place with no family except my daughter and myself. Life as a full-time adjunct university professor was very different than a life that included playdates, naps, and field trips.

Rebuilding after the storm is one thing, but rebuilding right in the middle of the storm feels next to impossible. Even in nature's storms, no construction company is going to start rebuilding any house while the winds are blowing, and the rain is falling. That would be ludicrous. In life's storms, however, it's absolutely necessary to rebuild in the middle of the storm. If we don't, we run the risk of being stuck in our pain, hurts, and turmoil, and carrying them with us indefinitely. If we don't start to rebuild in the middle of the storm, we will miss opportunities to grow and heal.

Hear me when I say this — rebuilding is *not* easy. There are going to be days when you feel like the last thing you want to do is get out of the bed and immerse yourself in the world and around people. I've been there. I'm an introvert so my need to be by myself was intensified. This often led to feelings of depression and anxiety. But please hear me when I say, it's completely possible and worth it to rebuild. Often, you rebuild stronger than you ever imagined you could be. The process of rebuilding, however, will look different for everyone.

After my divorce, I was thrown into survival mode. I did not necessarily view the upcoming years as a rebuilding process, but in hindsight, that is certainly what they became. I now was the primary and only constant parent in Jadyn's life. How would I navigate this? The door was left open figuratively for her father to walk through, but he did it when it was convenient for him and it had to fit his terms. Just a few short years later, he had already remarried for the third time and was living life with his new family, so her time spent with him was minimum at best. It truly was just Jadyn and me. I buckled down and knew that I had to not only heal myself, but I had to assist in her healing too. I would not allow this trauma to define either one of us. This meant keeping her in counseling for as long as she needed and giving her some leeway in allowing her to sort through her emotions. She was sad, confused, and anxious, and she needed space to sort through all of this in a loving and stable environment.

Rebuilding meant adjusting to not having a spouse I could lean on for anything. I did not have the convenience of relatives nearby, so I had to come up with contingency plans on how to navigate life alone. This meant having to be okay with the piled-up dishes, the unfolded laundry, eating out more frequently than I would prefer, and learning to set up boundaries so I would not wear myself out for all the tasks that now fell only on my shoulders. Everything from getting the oil changed in my vehicle to changing the air filters in my house to calling a repair man and hoping he wouldn't rip me off. (Yes, this almost happened!)

Rebuilding meant having to work two, sometimes three jobs, to make sure I stayed afloat and didn't get too far behind with unexpected bills. One surgery, one car repair, and one unexpected, but necessary trip could all, and did, set me back more than I liked. This also meant having to explain to my daughter that we couldn't do certain things she had grown accustomed to because "mom was on a budget." It meant telling her, "You'll have to wait until Mom gets paid."

Rebuilding meant trusting God with my next relationship. Not only would it impact me, but my daughter as well. Too many times we've turned on the news or had a friend or family member tell us that inappropriate actions occurred at the hands of a step-family member. This very thing happened to a sweet and dear friend of mine and I cannot fathom the unbearable pain she had to endure knowing her daughter had been violated in the most vicious way. Trusting another person to be a safe place to your child is terrifying. Hoping that potential new family members would not bring chaos and strife to the peace and stability I worked so hard to create in this new season was not enough. I needed to know what we rebuilt would be guarded and safe. These are just a few examples of the areas in which I had to rebuild. The outcome has been nothing but miraculous for me and I can only attribute the process to the amazing grace given to us by our Heavenly Father.

I have gone through divorce, miscarriage, infertility, anxiety, medical issues, depression, single parenting, and financial struggles. Some of these all at the same time and some are ongoing while writing this book. I'm so grateful that God spoke to me and gave me the strong desire to intentionally heal, not only for myself, which is most important, but also in order to help others as well. This hasn't come easy though. Not even a little bit. For every step I took forward at times, I felt like I got knocked back twenty. The examples I could give you are countless of these particular moments. Somedays I felt like I could run through the storm, but most days I truly felt like I was crawling. Can you relate?

Something that was very important to me in writing this book was that I come across as real and flawed and imperfect as possible — not fully put together. Many days, during the peak of my storm, I was tired of the sadness, I was exhausted from the crying, and I was exasperated from the constant emotional pain. I cried more tears in about a three-year timeframe than I felt like I cried my entire life (no exaggeration). I want you to know that what you've been feeling is okay. Please do not let anyone tell you otherwise. You are human, and we were all created with real and raw emotions. It's important you learn to feel your pain in order to get to the other side to peace.

Healing or rebuilding is a process with no set time limit on how long it will take. With divorce in particular, there are often constant reminders everywhere of the past life you once lived, which at times, feels like it can hinder your healing process. If there is a child or children involved, as there was in my case, you, more times than not, will have to stay in contact with your ex-spouse. If this person is toxic, then it can feel even more heart-wrenching. As your children get older and inevitably begin to share certain details about what your ex is doing in their life, even if you don't ask, this can be devastating to your heart. This can make it feel like healing will never happen. So how do you heal? In order to accomplish true healing, I feel confident in saying there are at least two things that are absolutely necessary.

First, God is waiting with open arms to have a relationship with you and He wants you to give Him your pain. He will meet you where you are. What do

I mean by that? Right now, in this moment, think of what you would consider your worst flaw. It may be something you've done, thought, or felt. Whatever it is, my dear friend, hear me when I say Jesus still loves you and is not mad at you. He doesn't hold your sins against you and He doesn't sit back amused at your suffering. Yes, no matter what it is, He truly loves you. God is love. Not only is He love, He is unconditional and unfailing love. Jeremiah 31:3 (NLT) states, *"Long ago the Lord said to Israel: "I have loved you, my people, with an everlasting love. With unfailing love I have drawn you to myself."*

I realize so many people have never experienced unconditional love so it's a foreign concept and feeling. I fall into this category. I have a biological father who's love and relationship with me has been very conditional. Unfortunately, because of that, I often have felt that way about people. But remember, God is not like man, so we have to try not to equate what we've experienced with people and think God treats us the same. God forgives. He gives us mercy and grace and favor every single day. He hurts when we hurt. He cries with us and for us.

Jesus unselfishly died on the cross so that we may live our best life possible. He died for us because He truly loves us. All He wants is a relationship with us. Salvation is here for you to take and hold on to. All you need to do is accept Jesus as your Lord and Savior. It's that simple. Jesus doesn't ask you to be perfect to accept Him. He doesn't ask you to change overnight. Sometimes, the message sent to people is that your life has to be flawless before you can have a relationship with Christ. Or the message is that God is mad at you for who you are or what you've done. Hear me when I say, that these are SO far from the truth! If you haven't already accepted Jesus as your Lord and Savior, let me guide you in a prayer. Read aloud the following:

Lord. I love you. Right here, in this moment, I acknowledge you, Jesus Christ, are God and that you came to earth to live a sinless life that I cannot live. I acknowledge that you died in my place so that I don't have to pay the penalty for what I deserve. I confess all my sin to you. Please forgive me. I am ready to trust you Jesus Christ as Lord and Savior. I ask that you come into my heart, take residence here, and begin living through me. Thank you, Lord. I love you.

My friend, I have some amazing news for you. If you truly believed what you just prayed, you are now saved by grace through Jesus Christ and are now a Christ follower. The angels in heaven are at this very moment rejoicing for *you*! And so am I!

You do not need to repeatedly say this prayer. It's a one and done deal. I know in this moment you may not necessarily feel any different, but let me assure you that you are. You are now guaranteed a spot in heaven for eternity with our Lord and Savior! That is worth celebrating!

Life doesn't just automatically change once you accept Jesus. Like anything else in life, it's a process. Please take it one day at time. Please do not make the mistake of feeling that you need to feel different in order for it to be real. Use this time to start getting to know Jesus a little bit more every single day. This is the first and ultimate step in rebuilding during your storm.

The second thing that needs to happen in order to go through the healing process is to not get pulled into the unfortunate negative stigma that exists in our society when it comes to receiving therapy or counseling. I am a living testimony that counseling works and I'm a strong believer in the benefits of it.

As a society, we have taken huge strides in accepting and bringing awareness to mental health. Unfortunately, there are still many people who choose to believe that counseling is not for them and that it will not benefit them. We have falsely believed that people who go to counseling are "crazy" or suffer from an extreme mental disorder, and many cultures believe it's best to keep their problems within their own families. These attitudes towards counseling are extremely damaging to us as individuals.

As a sociologist, I understand that many minority cultures in the United States do not believe in seeking counseling. We all carry around issues that can impact our mental health and simply our day-to-day activities. Race, ethnicity, and culture should not be a determinant as to whether or not we seek out professional help. I've heard time and time again from my minority students that wish to seek counseling that their families are not supportive or accepting of it. That is truly unfortunate. I hope by sharing my experience, that regardless of race, ethnicity, or even age, I can encourage you to start the process of seeking a counselor.

I first sought counseling for the first time during my separation. I was anxious and nervous, but I was encouraged by the research I had done on the benefits of counseling. I realize you may not even know where to begin in searching for a counselor. PsychologyToday.com is a great website to start your search or simply do a Google search for counselors in your area. You can narrow down your search by several different factors you feel are important to you such as the counselor's specialization, i.e. men issues, women issues, divorce, anxiety, depression, etc., and the counselor's gender, age, or religious background.

I look at the process of finding a counselor much like dating. You may have to try out a few different ones before you settle down with someone you're comfortable with. If the first session with the first counselor doesn't go the way you like, try again. I encourage you to not stop until you find one that you feel good about.

Please know that going to counseling is not like what is often portrayed on TV and in the movies. You simply are sitting in a comfortable setting with someone who has expertise in helping you navigate through the storm you are in. Most therapists allow you to lead and talk about what you want to talk about.

Sitting with someone who had the expertise to help guide me through the emotional process of divorce was priceless. If for no other reason but to have a positive, unbiased outlet, going to counseling truly helped me to heal. Often, we want to go to our friends to tell them everything that is going on in our lives with the hope they will give us good advice. There are a few things wrong with this. One, whether they realize it or not and no matter how hard they try, it may be very challenging for your friends to have an unbiased attitude towards your issues. Two, most do not have the professional training to give you the proper advice on how to truly heal. Lastly, I don't know a person who isn't dealing with their own issues, and if you're not careful, you will "dump" all your issues onto someone else not realizing you're adding more stress to them and not giving them anything in return. The lesson I learned from my therapy sessions, that I must acknowledge my pain and feel it in order to heal from it, was truly priceless. As much as I love my friends, none of them had the expertise to give me this invaluable advice.

If you have already begun the process of counseling, I commend you and I encourage you to keep going! If you've never tried it, regardless of how nervous you may be, remember that it often takes stepping out of your comfort zone to grow. I guarantee you won't regret it.

This life was not meant to be done alone. God has given us people in the form of family, friends, teachers, mentors, and yes, counselors or therapists, to help us through the most challenging parts of life. Please do not dismiss the importance of therapy. I'm proud to be an example, not only to my daughter, but also to my students and even my friends by letting them know I go to counseling. I have put my daughter in counseling at times when she was struggling with our divorce and I have witnessed the benefits for her. I have encouraged students to go as well. Those who have gone have not regretted it.

God wants to see you through all the storms of life. If you're a parent, stop for a moment and think about how you feel when your child is hurting. It could be the smallest scrape on the elbow to watching them lie in a hospital bed, but my guess is that you would trade places with them in a heartbeat. If you don't have kids, think of someone close to you and imagine the despair you feel when they hurt. Now try to multiply that by 1,000, or 10,000 or even 100,000. I don't know the exact number, but God feels our pain and hurts with us more than we could ever wrap our humanly minds around. Psalm 34:18 (NLT) says, *"The Lord is close to the brokenhearted; he rescues those whose spirits are crushed."*

Know that your life is an unending journey of change and growth. Change is often uncomfortable, but it doesn't have to have a negative outcome. When devastating hurricanes hit, they often ravage entire communities. The community eventually rebuilds though. Does the community look exactly the same as it did prior to the devastating hurricane? There may be some familiar sights but often, there is incredible change that has been brought about with a new-found stability and strength. You will rebuild. You will heal. Give yourself time. Give yourself the gift of experiencing the blessing God has for you that includes a beautiful and amazing life. It may not be the life you hoped for or planned, but I can promise you, in many ways, it will be better. God will not let you down. He will help you to rebuild —stronger than ever!

Chapter 6

Angels in the Storm

*See I am sending an angel ahead of you to guard you along the
way and to bring you to the place I have prepared.*
– Exodus 23:20 (NIV)

Surrounding yourself with the right people is
critical during a storm. Let me explain what I mean
when I say the "right" people. I'm confident in
saying that just because someone is related to you or
just because you've known the person most of your
life, does not necessarily mean they are the right
person to help you through your storm. This is not to
minimize the relationship you have with your sister,
brother, your mom or dad, or even your best friend. I
simply mean just because we call someone family or
friend does not mean they can be there for you in the
way you need during your storm.

Your first initial thought may very well be, "Well,
my best friend and I have known each other for the
past thirty years so of course I expect her to be there
for me!" Please be mindful that time does not define
a person's ability to give you the emotional support
you will need during a storm. Not every person that
was with me in my storm was part of my life for a
long time period of time.

Discernment is the ability to judge something or someone well. Not judge in the negative sense, but in a way that allows you to know whether something or somebody is good for you. True discernment comes by including God in your decisions. Ask Him to guide the right people to you. Ask Him to reveal things to you that will hinder and help your growth and healing.

There were a few things that really helped me in knowing who should and shouldn't be a part of my inner circle during my storm. The first was to have a very real and honest talk with myself regarding people's perspectives and attitude towards life. Ask yourself a few questions.

"Does this person have a positive or negative attitude most of the time?" The last thing you need at this moment is to be around someone who views the world through a negative lens. Proverbs 17:22 (NLT) reads, *"A cheerful heart is good medicine, but a broken spirit saps a person's strength."*

Next, "Is this person complaining about something most of the time you talk?" When you're not in the middle of a storm, you have a higher capacity to deal with other people's grievances. Whether we realize it or not, we can build up an immunity so to speak to our friends' negativity and write it off as, "that's just how so and so is." Now is not the time. Now is the time to learn to be a bit selfish and take care of yourself, although by no means do I think of self-care as being selfish. You must seek out and surround yourself with positivity.

Ask yourself whether or not your friends are always in agreement with you. We all want someone to tell us we're right for our feelings and behaviors, especially if we feel like we've been wronged, but an authentic friend will call you on stuff even when you don't necessarily want to hear it. Telling you what you need to hear, however, always needs to come from a place of love otherwise it can add more stress, hurt, and anger to an already difficult situation. If these people are genuine in their relationship with you, you will know that all constructive criticism is given in love.

Lastly, and probably most importantly, "Does this person truly believe and more importantly, have a relationship with God?" This is important because if they do, automatically, they will be someone who is going to give you a different and beneficial perspective on life —a perspective that will aid in your healing. Please notice I said "relationship" and not "religious." Having a relationship with God is a lot different in many aspects than just saying you're religious. If a person has a one-on-one personal relationship with Christ, the person will approach your storm with sensitivity, humility, and the care you need (Colossians 3:12). Now is not the time where you need someone to remind you how badly you messed up, condemn you, and throw scriptures at you to make you repent. The loving demonstration of Jesus' love will help in the healing of all people. Much like Jesus in John 11:33-35, compassion is what you need and deserve.

In the middle of my separation and divorce, one of my angels, my friend, Arlene, who I'll talk more about soon, told me something that did not feel good in the moment to hear, but it was truly what I needed to hear. Because I knew Arlene's heart and that she genuinely cared for me, I received her advice with as much grace as I could muster up. On one particular emotionally tough day, since she lived right down the street, I called her to see if she could meet me for a quick vent and walk. I quickly told her what was going on and what had me in tears. After thoughtfully listening, she stopped me and said, "Favor, you're making this about you and it's not. This is about him and what he needs to sort out. Stop making it about you." Ouch! But that ouch only lasted for about ten seconds. I processed what she said, and it made all the sense in the world. Later on, once I uncovered I was indeed married to a narcissist, I realized just how spot on she was with her words. That advice stayed with me and helped me emotionally even to this day as I write, two years post-divorce.

Also, in looking for the right people, ask yourself what do you do during the majority of your interaction with them? Are you talking about or gossiping about other people, even other family members? (Life lesson #123: if they're gossiping about other people, it's a matter of time before you're next on the list. Don't really know if it's lesson #123, but it sounds good!) Please understand that I am not saying that every time you're together you need to be memorizing the Ten Commandments, Psalm 23, and the whole book of Revelations. I'm simply saying the conversation and interaction should be one that are fruitful, positive, and uplifting, rather than gossipy, negative, and discouraging.

Dear friend, the point I hope you're receiving from this is your circle of friends should be there to remind you that you're stronger than you feel. They're there to make you smile and laugh. They're there to be that shoulder you need to cry on. They're there to just share a space with you when there's simply no words that will help. They're there to remind you just how special you are and how needed you are. They're there to remind you that the sun *will* shine again. They're even there to lovingly tell you when you've messed up. Most importantly, they're there to remind you of God's unconditional love.

One day I was talking with a client of mine about relationships. She proceeded to tell me about a podcast she listened to in which one of the main points was that when a couple gets married, often times one of the spouses looks to the other spouse to be their everything. Ladies can be especially guilty of this. We expect our spouse to fulfill that role that, prior to getting married, five or six girlfriends occupied. One person cannot be your everything. The only one Who is and can and wants to be your everything is God. It's unfair to other people and it's unfair to yourself to expect that from any other living, flawed human being. We've all heard it said before, people will always disappoint you. This is true because not one of us is without sin (Roman

3:10). That being said, God will send angels to you who can be there for you at the right time, in the right way, for the right amount of time.

As I previously mentioned, Arlene was truly one of my angels. I selfishly believe that her time spent in Texas as my neighbor and very good friend was because God knew I would need her. God knew our time together would be short, but it has been, to date, one of the most impactful friendships I have ever had. Not only was she my friend, but she was probably one of the few women that I truly looked up to and found myself wanting to emulate. Arlene is that person who speaks to everyone! She wipes down the counters in the bathroom at a restaurant left wet by other people (I've seen her do it) and she finds a way to make every person she encounters liven up. A beautiful woman inside and out, a wonderful wife, a retired veteran, and just a flat our hilarious girlfriend! People like Arlene are unique and special and I'm forever grateful to God He felt I was worthy of her friendship.

She and her family moved into their home about three to four months after my ex-husband and I moved into our home. I met them while out on a run and our friendship quickly developed from there. After I moved out of my home, she and her family were set to relocate out-of-state about six months later. What are the odds that we both had a beautiful home built in the same subdivision, around the same time, and bonded the way we did only to have neither of us living in that subdivision anymore a short five years later?

Arlene was there to allow me to vent and cry about my divorce and pick up my daughter, so I could have an hour or so to myself. She was that friend that didn't ask, she just did, because she knew I needed it. She would call me and say, "Favor, I'm ten minutes away! Tell Jadyn to put her shoes on so she can go have dinner with us!" I smile and laugh, and literally cry a bit, as I think about that, but she knew she held that space with me and I truly love her for that. As I'm writing about these friendships, I'm not fighting back my tears too well because her friendship literally makes me feel Gods love. That is a sign that you have the right people in your circle. God loved me enough to send me exactly who I needed at the right time. He sent me an angel in my friend, Arlene. Like I mentioned, Arlene and I are now separated by distance, but in some ways our friendship has grown stronger. We can't take for granted any longer that we live one minute from each other, so we now must be intentional about staying in contact. But I'm confident that what God planted in our friendship will carry us a lifetime.

Most people have good intentions, but sometimes as great as those intentions are, they may not be what you need at this particular time. Again, I repeat, no disrespect towards the people you love most in the world, but self-care is one of your highest priorities and some of that self-care involves being very selective about who is closest to you in the middle of your storm.

There are many questions you need to ask yourself in regard to who needs to be in your circle at this point in time. Let me just stop here and say that I truly believe this circle needs to be small. I'm an empath and a high-level introvert, so I'm naturally comfortable around just a few people and have always just had a small circle of people who I consider close. I realize though that there is a world full of extroverts, and those who occupy a space in the middle, and a small circle of friends is just not how they operate. My challenge to both types of people is this: push yourself to be uncomfortable for just a while knowing that this challenge will aid in your healing. Introverts, you will want to seclude yourself from all people, but challenge yourself to stay in touch with even just two people on a regular basis. Extroverts, you will want to surround yourself with tons of people, but challenge yourself to limit the number to your top two or three friends. Too many people are just as harmful as no people. Find your close-knit circle and allow them to be the angels that God will amazingly bless you with.

My circle during my storm included about four people. Each person uplifted me in a different way that contributed to my overall well-being. My prayer partner was just that and I know even as I begin to write about him, my words won't do justice to how much I appreciate him. I could email him at 2 p.m. or 2 a.m. just to vent about where I was spiritually, and he got it. He would pray on my behalf at the drop of a dime, no questions asked, as well as send me scripture. God used him like I have never seen God use anyone before. If I was "off" spiritually, my prayer partner knew it. He introduced me to Bible verses that contributed greatly to my healing, not only spiritually, but emotionally as well. It was also refreshing to have a male in my life whose friendship was 100% platonic, genuine, and spiritual. He constantly reminded me that God loved me and as each day passed, I felt God's love grow inside me more and more each and every day. To this day, I call him my angel. Our friendship was, and is, so unlikely, yet God loved me enough to bring this person to me at the time I would need his friendship the most.

Another friend was there to help me with his physical presence in so many ways — ways I cannot repay. This friend helped me move out of the house that my ex-husband had left. There was much to be packed and dumped that had accumulated over a sixteen-year marriage and my ex-husband left my daughter and I to take care of all of it ourselves. At the time, I lived in a 5,000-plus square foot home so I had a task in front of me! Not only was there the physical labor of packing and moving, I was also still trying to manage my emotions from the divorce all while trying to hold it together for my daughter. (The wind and rain of this storm was picking up during this particular time. Can you hear the winds howling?)

This beautiful friendship eventually grew into more and at the time I write this book, I am blessed to call this friend, not only my best friend, but my boyfriend. Qasim and I have a bond like I've never experienced before. Personally, I don't like to compare one relationship to another, but it's important to note that I have for the most part, only been in one long-term relationship. I got married to my ex-husband two weeks after I turned twenty years old and spent sixteen years married to him. Prior to that, I was a college student dating. All that said, I truly know that what "Q" and I shared was something special.

Q and I, unfortunately, were going through divorces simultaneously before we began our relationship, so we had the added challenge of healing ourselves from our previous relationships. Many people, experts, religious authorities, authors, etc. have written on the fact that a person should wait "x" amount of time before they begin a new relationship. In a nutshell, the longer you've been in a relationship, the longer you should wait seems to be the consensus. Let me say I am no expert when it comes to relationships. I don't fully disagree with these experts. I do think this timeframe will look different for every person, however. I also believe there needs to be some *intentional* personal work done on yourself if you do choose to start a new relationship shortly after another one has ended. This is not only fair to yourself, but to your new partner. Your relationship will implode if you do not do the necessary work individually. This looks different for every person, but for me personally this included a diligent and intentional prayer life, attending church, going to counseling, and having time to myself. Be fair to yourself and your new partner and do the hard work up front so you do not damage your new relationship.

Going through my divorce was one of the toughest times in my life. I cried myself to sleep more nights than I can count. I had just as many, if not more, sleepless nights. Waking up at three 'o clock in the morning was becoming my norm. I want to end this chapter by saying this and please hear me on this. God places angels in our lives in order to help us, grow us, care for us, love us, and often to take care of us in a season that would turn out dramatically different if they weren't sent by God. As blessed as I was to have had and still have angels in my life, please remember our ultimate Angel — our heavenly Father. No human can give to us what He can. As much as Arlene, my prayer partner, and my boyfriend all helped me to grow in many ways, and as much as I love and adore all of them, all of them together come nowhere close to how much God cared for me. We're all flawed. We all sin. We all are dealing with life as it comes, often knocking us off balance at times. God is perfect. His care and love are perfect. And His grace is sufficient enough to carry us through our storms.

Chapter 7

Smile In Your Storm

If you look to Him for help, He will put a smile on your face. You will have no need to be ashamed. – Psalm 34:5 (ERV)

One thing I have learned to love about storms is the weather that follows. Many storms end with beautiful weather that literally feels quite perfect. It's never too hot or too cold. Sometimes there's a light breeze and the sun is shining like nothing ever happened. No matter how loud, terrifying, or intimidating that storm was, I always find myself breathing a little easier after. After the storms of life, I find myself doing a lot of reflecting. I might ask, "Did I prepare to the best of my ability? What can I do differently the next time a storm comes? How can I be better prepared for the next time?" Most importantly, I look for lessons. I don't ever want anything in my life to be wasted. I want to make sure I do my best to not make the same mistakes twice or to make sure I can prepare to the best of my ability for the next storm.

I realize that some storms will come out of nowhere and all we can do is hope that we're prepared. We can board up our windows, lock down furniture so it doesn't blow away, put ten flashlights and several candles in our home, but sometimes when that storm hits, it finds a way to still knock everything out no matter how prepared we try to be.

Unlike nature's storms, we often do not get a forecast of the personal storms that will hit us. Yet, similar to a nature's storm, when a storm does hit, I can't just immediately, in a moment's notice, decide to pack up my house and move to another city. That just seems silly, right? And truthfully, there really never is enough time. What I can do, however, is prepare myself for the future storms that will come my way. How do I do that? Glad you asked! I have learned to SMILE in my storms.

> **S — Stop and Pray**
> **M — Meditate on God's Word**
> **I — Inspire Others**
> **L — Listen for Direction**
> **E — Enjoy His Presence, Power, & Provision**

S — Stop and Pray

Most people I know who have been through a storm realize just how powerless they truly are in their own human ability when compared to the strength of the ravaging winds and torrential down pours. There's no stopping a storm. When it comes, it comes. My storm knocked me right into the arms of my loving God and for that I am truly grateful. I have been a Christian for as long as I can remember. I have prayed more times than I care to count. I have seen God work in my life and in the life of others. But it wasn't until the darkest period of my life that I truly strengthened my relationship with Christ. That alone, makes every tear and every sleepless night completely worth it.

For some of your reading this, that may not make sense. How on earth could you go through a divorce after a sixteen-year marriage, endure the pain of your ex-husband being with a former employee, get pregnant after struggling with infertility only to have a miscarriage, have conflict with your ex-husband, surgery, and be taken to court all in a two-year timeframe and say that it was all worth it, Favor? Easy. Stopping to pray in the middle of my storm allowed me to turn over every burden I could not carry, and it released me from having to figure everything out for myself. It wasn't easy and certainly not without enduring much pain, but leaning on God made it easier. God *will* carry your burdens for you if you allow Him to. But first you must humble yourself through prayer and talk to God about what it is you need from Him. He will listen, and He will help. First John 5:14 (NIV) reminds us, *"This is the confidence we have in approaching God: that if we ask for anything according to His will, He hears us."* Amen!

I have experienced God answering my prayers. There are two things I want to say in reference to this. One, experiencing God answering your prayers, if you haven't yet, is one of the most amazing experiences you will have. To hear very specifically from God and to experience a close relationship with Him brings about a peace and freedom that is unlike anything else. Do not mistake what I mean by this though. It would be irresponsible of me to not tell you something in regard to that, which is the second thing. Sometimes we have a very specific prayer and want it answered a specific way. Yet, when it doesn't get answered in that very specific way, we automatically equate that to God not hearing or answering our prayer. God loves us so much that He truly wants what is best for us and our minds may not be able to comprehend what His best is. We may not understand until later that the way God answered our prayer was exactly how it needed to be answered.

Sadly, so many people treat God like a genie in a bottle. God does not operate that way. He simply wants a relationship with us. Building a relationship with God I can assure you will definitely be worth it. If you're not quite sure how to do it, start simply by praying and talking to God. Be open and honest. He understands.

M — Meditate on God's Word

It's hard to build a relationship with someone you don't really know. Think about that for a second. When you started a new romantic relationship, you wanted nothing more to know everything about the person you were with. What makes them laugh, what makes them angry, what makes them sad, and whether or not they snore at night.

How did you come across this information? I would be willing to guess that you learned all of this by building a relationship with them, spending time with them, and paying very close attention to all the nuances about them. Why should we expect things to be any different with our Creator who knows us better than anybody?

In order to learn more about God, we must dive into His word. It's as simple as that. I feel compelled to share something at this very moment while I write this book. Know that there are many versions of the Bible that exist. The Word is the same, but the words inside the actual Bible may read very differently depending on which version you read. Many people who may not be completely familiar with the Bible may automatically assume, and in turn be turned off, by the "old school" version known as the King James Version. For many people, attempting to read this version with its many "thouest" and "believieth" type of words is an automatic turn off. Admittedly, it's not my go to either. I suggest trying some of the other versions to help your reading experience become better understood and yes, even enjoyable. There is the frequently used New International Version (NIV), the New Living Translation (NLT) and two of my favorites have become the Easy Read Version (ERV) and The Message (MSG). For me, the latter two especially have broken down some difficult to read scriptures in the King James Version and they all of a sudden clicked for me just by simply changing the Bible version.

Remember, God's Word is God's Word. Please do not make the mistake of thinking the different versions change what is to be conveyed. When I lecture on sociological concepts in my college classroom, I use certain verbiage that I know a college-aged student will understand. When I explain the same concept to maybe a middle schooler, I change my words. The meaning and definition of what I'm saying hasn't changed. It's the same thing with the different versions of the Bible.

There is no so called "right" way to read and study God's Word. Please do not let anyone fool you into thinking that you are less than or your relationship with God isn't "right" or can't be valid if you decide to not do it their way. Their way may include sitting for thirty minutes or longer straight with no interruptions and reading non-stop. If that works for you, great. If not, that's absolutely fine. Just as an example, there have been plenty of moments where I carved out thirty minutes to sit and read my Bible hoping to hear from God. I didn't always. There were other times where I was about to go to sleep, but decided to read my Bible for a quick five or ten minutes and heard from God clear as day. The key is to just start somewhere. Read the same verse over and over again if that's what you need to do to get yourself in a rhythm. You will grow in this area the more you do it. And you'll thank yourself that you did.

I — Inspire Others
Many of us have heard the phrase, "Hurt people hurt people." Well the opposite is also true — helping people helps people. Helping people is a natural healer. I'm a living example of this. Little did I know God was setting me up to be in an amazing position while going through one of my biggest storms of my

life. I started teaching in January of 2016 after not having worked for the previous ten years during which I was a full-time, stay-at-home mom and full-time student working on my graduate degree. My ex-husband and I separated two months later in March of 2016. I barely was able to get my feet wet in this job I worked so hard to achieve before I was forced to try to balance the excitement of a dream job with feelings of depression and overwhelming sadness.

I would have never guessed that during one of the most difficult times emotionally in my life that God would give me the ability and willingness to help so many people the way I have. Many days, helping myself along with my daughter was a task that I felt like I was barely accomplishing well. So often during this time, I wanted to just lie in bed and not do anything, but cry. So many nights were sleepless and filled with anxiety, so finding enough energy to function during the day on four hours of sleep at best was extremely challenging.

I was, and am, beyond blessed to work a job that I absolutely love, which made it that much easier to get up in the morning, no matter how stressful my personal life. This is absolutely, without a doubt, because of God. It brought me so much joy to be able to inspire my students each time I stepped foot inside my classroom. It humbled me when students emailed me to tell me how encouraged they were by a lecture I had given. And being ranked the top professor on the website, Rate My Professor, wasn't too shabby either. I say that with all humility, but I bring it up because it blows me away that I was able to have a positive influence in my students' lives when simultaneously my personal life was in shambles. Only God!

In October of 2018, right in the middle of my storm, God gave me the thought and idea to start my mentoring group called Fit For Your Purpose. We had our first official gathering in January of 2019! I started this group with the full intention of sowing into the lives of the young ladies, however, the residual gift of joy I received from giving to the young ladies was one of the most amazing blessings I could ask for.

God may not be calling you to necessarily start a mentoring group, so I encourage you to find other ways to give back to other people during your storm. This may seem like the *very* last thing you want to do right now. I get that. I don't expect you to just drop this book at this very moment and go start feeding the homeless. But I do challenge you to find ways to give back even if it's just an hour a week. Let me elaborate more on why this is so important.

First and foremost, God commands this of us. Galatians 6:2 (ERV) states, *"Help each other with your troubles. When you do this, you are obeying the law of Christ."* Like I mentioned, I know if you're in the middle of your storm, there's a real possibility this is the last thing you can imagine doing when most days seem like you can barely take care of yourself. My friend, this simply means you're human. God created us, so He knows the benefit of helping others. There are an endless number of people who walk around who need help in some sort of way. It may be in a tangible way, it may be in a physical way, or even in an emotional way. Helping someone in a tangible way doesn't always have to equate to something extreme such as emptying out your bank account. It may be as simple as buying a $2.00 cup of coffee for that co-worker you know seems a little down today. Helping someone in a physical way can be assisting an elderly person at the grocery story put their groceries in their car and taking their shopping cart back into the store. Helping someone in an emotional way doesn't mean that you need to muster up enough energy to try to give them advice. That can simply be sharing a quiet space with them — simply sitting with them. God commands us to help others to help them yet in His amazing sovereignty, He knows helping others will also help ourselves.

God knows that when we help others it takes the attention off of our own problems and truly helps us to feel better. Luke 6:38 (ERV) reads, *"Give to others and you will receive. You will be given much. It will be poured into your hands –more than you can hold. You will be given so much that it will spill into your lap. The way you give to others is the way God will give to you."* We tend to often think of the materialistic things that God will bless us with, and He will do that too, but I wholeheartedly feel that He's also referring to a blessing that is not tangible — emotional healing.

I encourage you to dig deep, even in your storm, and reap the blessings that come from inspiring others.

L — Listen for Direction

We all get lost from time to time. That's a part of life. You may have actually experienced being physically lost or you may have experienced feeling lost on which way to go in life. That may be in a relationship, do I stay, or do I go? — a job, do I take this new job offer or wait for a better one? or a major purchase, is it time to upgrade to a new car or can my old car last another 10,000 miles? When we're lost, we need direction. There is only One who can give us direction that is guaranteed to never lead us down the wrong path.

God will not leave you stranded in your storm. Psalms 32:8 (NIV) states, *"I will instruct you and teach you in the way you should go. I will counsel you with my loving eye on you."* I'll be the first to admit, when you are in the eye of your storm, when life is bringing about more stressors than you feel like you can possibly handle, it seems like God is a million miles away. You pray endlessly, you cry, you vent, you scream, and often it feels like no one is on the other end to receive these heartfelt emotions. But God is listening. God cares. God will not let your pain be wasted.

God wants to be our go-to. He doesn't want our go-to to be people or things, although they have a place after Him. He wants us to put all of our trust in Him. Sometimes it's easier said than done. Let's be real. In the initial days or weeks of our storms, it can be downright difficult to put all our trust in Him. I'm saying this because in all my years of being a Christ follower, I want you to know that I experienced these very real feelings. I sometimes had wished I knew that other Christ followers were having those same feelings, so I would not have been so hard on myself about the doubt I was experiencing. I learned in my storm that it's okay to have those feelings. God is not mad at us for doubting. He understands. But in order to know what God wants us to do and how He wants us to do it, we have to listen.

E—Enjoy His Presence, Power, & Provision

My amazing friend, Arlene, was by far one of my favorite people to be around during my storm. She's genuine, she's hilarious, she's caring and compassionate, and she's real. Every time I left her presence, I felt energized, renewed, and uplifted, and she wasn't even trying. I can't speak for everyone, but in my humble opinion, there's nothing like being in the presence of someone you have an amazing relationship with. For you, that may be your best friend or your spouse. It could be your children, or it could be a mentor. Either way, the laughter, the comradery, the compassion, and the joy you experience by just simply being around this person is priceless. That's how God feels about us when we make time for Him. He also wants us to feel that way about Him too.

I have grown to truly love my quiet times I spend with God. During my storm, when it was often easy for me to want to be alone, I can say my quiet times were invaluable to me. I can't say that every time I had my quiet moments I had an earth-shattering moment of feeling His presence, but I did enjoy reading His Word and applying it to my life. I loved reading about His promises and how He would not let anyone take advantage of me. I loved reading how His love for me was unconditional when I hadn't always felt that from people. He would often validate His Word to me through different moments during my storm. God doesn't expect us to just spend every waking moment in "quiet time" with Him, but He does desire for us to get to know Him on a very personal level. You won't regret these moments and will come to enjoy His presence, just like you do with that amazing friend.

As you begin to spend more time with God, not only will you enjoy His presence, but you also will recognize His power and His provision. I mentioned in a previous chapter that my ex-husband took me to court in which I had to find a lawyer in less than twenty-four hours. It was nothing but for God's power and provision that I made it through those dreadful few days. God showed His amazing power by not letting my enemy win. Exodus 15:6 (NLT) states, *"Your right hand, O Lord, is glorious in power. Your right hand, O Lord, smashes the enemy."* Please understand. Just like any relationship, a relationship with God cannot be one-sided. God desires to have a mutual relationship with us. If you're only calling on God to take away your enemies, but you don't give Him the honor and praise He so desires and deserves, you're unfortunately treating Him like the genie in the bottle that He is so far from. God truly showed up with His power and provisions in that I had just enough money in my savings account to pay for a lawyer. Praise be to God for His presence, power, and provision.

To SMILE through your storm may seem like the very last thing you want to do. I get that better than anybody. I cried more tears than I could have ever thought imaginable. I felt depressed to the point that everything I typically enjoyed doing felt like a chore. I was constantly tired, both physically and mentally. My life felt much like what Job expresses in Job 10 (MSG):

> "I can't stand my life—I hate it!
> I'm putting it all out on the table,
> all the bitterness of my life—I'm holding back nothing."

Job prayed:

> "Here's what I want to say:
> Don't, God, bring in a verdict of guilty
> without letting me know the charges you're bringing.
> How does this fit into what you once called 'good'—
> giving me a hard time, spurning me,
> a life you shaped by your very own hands,
> and then blessing the plots of the wicked?
> You don't look at things the way we mortals do.
> You're not taken in by appearances, are you?
> Unlike us, you're not working against a deadline.
> You have all eternity to work things out.
> So what's this all about, anyway—this compulsion

to dig up some dirt, to find some skeleton in my
closet?
You know good and well I'm not guilty.
You also know no one can help me."
"You made me like a handcrafted piece of
pottery—
and now are you going to smash me to pieces?
Don't you remember how beautifully you worked
my clay?
Will you reduce me now to a mud pie?
Oh, that marvel of conception as you stirred
together
semen and ovum—
What a miracle of skin and bone,
muscle and brain!
You gave me life itself, and incredible love.
You watched and guarded every breath I took.
"But you never told me about this part.
I should have known that there was more to it—
That if I so much as missed a step, you'd notice
and pounce,
wouldn't let me get by with a thing.
If I'm truly guilty, I'm doomed.
But if I'm innocent, it's no better—I'm still
doomed.
My belly is full of bitterness.
I'm up to my ears in a swamp of affliction.
I try to make the best of it, try to brave it out,
but you're too much for me,
relentless, like a lion on the prowl.
You line up fresh witnesses against me.
You compound your anger

and pile on the grief and pain!"
"So why did you have me born?
I wish no one had ever laid eyes on me!
I wish I'd never lived — a stillborn,
buried without ever having breathed.
Isn't it time to call it quits on my life?
Can't you let up, and let me smile just once
Before I die and am buried,
before I'm nailed into my coffin, sealed in the
ground,
And banished for good to the land of the dead,
blind in the final dark?"

Can you relate to this?? Boy, could I ever! Job is most known in the Bible for having everything he loved and cared for stripped away from him. How on earth could a loving God allow all of this to happen? How could a loving God allow a miscarriage after years of infertility? How could my seemingly happy marriage end up in shattered pieces, and my ex-husband and I become the worse of enemies? How could I get through each day with my daughter dealing with anxiety and tears? How could I get through the financial struggles I was facing as a single mom?

How can the world be filled with so much hate? How could children be committing suicide at higher rates due to cyberbullying? How can so many people, including children, die from mass shootings? God, how do we smile in all of this turmoil? Through all of these storms of life, God is there. He has never left us. We've left Him. He wants us back. God wants to help you feel whole again. He will help you in miraculous ways that you didn't even know were possible.

Imagine yourself for just a moment standing on top of a mountain looking down at all the things and people that you feel took something from you. You feel anger, disgust, confusion, anxiety, sadness, hurt, disappointment, and yes, even hate. Now I want you to think about each of those same things and people, and think about how you became stronger in spite of them. This may be a first for you. It's so easy to spend much of our time focused on the all that has gone wrong that we don't spend one moment on what has gone right. If you can think of just one positive that came out of a negative, that is a blessing. I guarantee you that you're stronger in one way or another. You may not feel it, but I guarantee you that you are absolutely stronger than you feel. I know that because you're reading this book, which means you're still standing.

Now imagine yourself standing on top of the same mountain looking up to the sky. There are no more clouds, rain, or hail. The sky is a calming blue and the breeze that's passing over you feels amazing. The storm has calmed and you're still standing. There is no more rain in your storm. This is where God is taking you. This is where God wants to take you. Please do not give up before you reach this moment. If it hasn't already, it will come. I promise. The key is to surrender your life to Christ and allow

Him to take control of your life just like He desires. It *will* be worth it. You have absolutely *nothing* to lose!

Life is not promised to us without storms. In fact, just as much as we are promised air in our body to breathe, the same can be said for storms. Storms are where we grow though. Storms are painful; they drain us, physically and emotionally. The rain that falls from the sky is often in close competition with the tears that fall from our eyes. Your storm may be temporary, or it may be ongoing. Regardless of time, God is right there to see you through. And once you get through the loud booms of the thunder, the hail that is knocking on your windows, and the torrential rain that seems to never let up, you, my friend, will find yourself reigning in your storm.

Conclusion

From Rain to Reign

From the Lord comes deliverance. May your blessing be on your people. — Psalms 3:8 (NIV)

As I conclude this book, it's approximately two years from the first time I began writing it. God placed an amazing topic and title on my heart and truly guided me through the process of completion. The completion of this book is a testimony to what God will do in your life. I had so many doubts through the process wondering if I could write a book, get it published, and it serve the purpose that I hoped — which simply was to help heal people. I'm sure there is at least one big thing in your life that you've been wondering if you can accomplish. Let me be the first to tell you if nobody else has already said it — yes you can! It won't always be easy or happen overnight, but with patience and perseverance, it can happen. Yes, it's been a challenge to get a book done when most of my time is spent working two jobs, and every now and again, three. But God helped me to be able to find time and for that I am eternally grateful.

I have worn the single mom hat boldly and proudly in that I have committed to be the very best mom I could be to my daughter. For me, this meant making sure she knew she was always my priority. If I had to turn down jobs because it would cause me to miss too many of her games or miss work because she was sick, then so be it. I trusted God to provide in those moments, and He always did. And no, waiting on Him to provide was not always easy to do. I have been the only consistent parent in her life and I take on that responsibility very seriously. Life involves many 4:30 a.m. or 5:00 a.m. wake-up days, driving her about thirty to forty-five minutes away to her school during the week, being there for her emotionally and physically, showing up at her games and plays, all while hoping that pile of laundry will somehow learn to fold itself (it never did!)

Despite the exhaustion that life has brought the past few years, I have learned some solid, godly life lessons that I hope will give you a new perspective in your storm. One of the first is this: the pain in your life truly has a purpose. In order to really illustrate this, I have to go back about thirty years to about the age of nine or ten. I don't look back at my childhood with thoughts of wishing I could be a kid again. There were decent moments, but much of my childhood memories are filled with fear, anxiety, frustration, and sadness. I grew up scared of my dad, never knowing what was going to set him off into some uncontrollable rage. Unfortunately, my brother received the brunt of his anger, but I can still remember the screams of my brother as he was beaten by my father. At 6'6", my dad seemed like an angry and scary giant to my nine or ten-year old self. To this day, I can't understand how a father can be so angry and mean to his daughter (or any father toward any of his children for that matter). I can still remember getting in trouble for what felt to be the smallest things, especially since I was too fearful to misbehave. I can remember being a senior in high school and literally counting down the days to move out and go away to college.

Fast forward, I made the decision to get married at twenty years old. I was always mature for my age and obviously felt like I could handle such a big responsibility. Yet, I know my upbringing of not having a father who was empathetic and truly there for me emotionally, played a role in me gravitating towards a long-term relationship so early. I understand from a personal and professional point of view that young ladies need a positive, caring, loving, male figure in their life early. Just because a man is present in the home, doesn't mean you're getting what you need from that relationship.

Why do I bring up my past as I'm ending this book? Simple. This book wouldn't be had I not gone through everything I've gone through in life, starting with my foundation. My father being the way he was actually made me the mom I am today. I knew without a shadow of a doubt that I didn't want my daughter growing up being fearful and hating her childhood. I wanted her to always know she could come to me with anything and I wanted her to enjoy being around me as much as I enjoy being around her.

Much of my book is centered around the past few years of my life when I was going through a divorce. By no means am I saying that I'm grateful for my divorce. I am saying that through my pain and hurt, this book has come about. If my pain, my story, and my journey will help another person navigate their storm, then I take on that pain wholeheartedly. Life is going to bring us storms. What we do with them is up to us.

Another life lesson: looking for the blessings in the storm has to be very intentional. There will be days where you don't want to "work" at getting better or simply put, you just don't have the energy. You'll experience anger, frustration, and yes, even hatred towards individuals who sought to intentionally cause you harm. I've experienced that feeling so often and my guess is you have to. Yet, many mornings I committed to waking up to sit quietly while talking to God and meditating on His Word. It helped me in reflecting on all His goodness and the goodness in my life. But guess what? There were days when I would do that and God felt so distant and far and quiet and I was left feeling angry, sad, and hurt. It's okay to feel that way. You just can't stay there. Commit to feeling the pain, but working to constantly moving forward.

Looking for the blessing means no matter how angry I get because of the pain and damage caused by my ex-husband, I'm eternally grateful for the extremely tight bond my daughter and I have built. If not for the fact that I'm her mom, and that takes precedence, I could easily say she's my best friend.

God couldn't have blessed me with a better daughter. In a time when many teenagers want to spend their time only online, streaming, or texting, I count my blessings that my now fourteen-year-old daughter still loves to snuggle up next to me and watch a movie or enjoys going with me to work, even on her days off of school when she could be home sleeping in. I do believe that we would have been close despite the trials and storms of divorce, but there is no doubt that this particular storm definitely pushed us closer together.

In the midst of writing this book, my boyfriend and I struggled in our relationship. We both brought baggage into this new relationship and it was starting to rear its ugly head. We were together yet many days we felt so distant. Our relationship reached a climatic point one weekend where I had decided I was done. In the midst of trying to heal the wounds from my past relationship, the brokenness of this relationship was just too much to deal with anymore. But something changed in my boyfriend that weekend. I continued to pray for him, but I knew the heavy lifting, so to speak, had to come from God. And it did. After months of us both working and being very intentional about our healing process, we are stronger than we have ever been. God wanted us to trust Him with our relationship, and we did. The result? Not just a stronger romantic relationship, but a friendship that is truly amazing. I am grateful for a boyfriend, best friend, and partner who is willing to work on himself and doesn't allow pride to keep him from growing.

I'm grateful that God continues to speak to me on the areas I need to grow in as well.

I hope by reading this book you are reminded of God's amazing and unconditional love. It's easy to know and feel that when life is going smoothly, but it's in those dark moments when the clouds are a shade away from being black that we need this reminder. Where would we be without God's amazing love? God did not leave me to fend for myself in the biggest storm of my life and He will not leave you either. That's a promise I can make. Even in the moments when I did not feel His presence or hear His voice, I had grown enough in my faith that I knew He was there and that there was a reason for me to go through the tough moments. Now let me pause here and say this did not happen overnight and I'm still a work in progress.

Many of us have an innate need to know the reasons why we go through things. One of the many lessons God revealed to me was that certain things in life may not be for me to know. And that is something we all have to learn to be okay with. First Corinthians 2:11 (ERV) reminds us that *"no one knows God's thoughts except God's spirit."* What if that unbearable circumstance you went through was to help someone else? That someone may be a stranger, a person close to you presently, or it may even be family members who will come later in life that you may never have the privilege of meeting. What if our storm is that circumstance that leads us to a very real and personal relationship with the One who created us? What if our storm needed to happen in order to get us one step closer to our final home, in eternity with Jesus Christ?

Another goal I had in writing this book was to share my very real fears, thoughts, and concerns that entered my mind during my storm. There's power in being vulnerable which aids in helping someone else. When I stand before my students and teach, it's often the personal stories I share that allows them to connect the material more than just the words out of a textbook.

I mentioned earlier in this book that I love to read and that I was constantly trying to find books that would help to alleviate the pain. I started to notice that it seemed much of my reading came from people who seemed to already have their life "together." I am not saying those particular books didn't serve a purpose, but sometimes these books made me feel that I was nowhere close to where I was trying to be, and I felt like they were hindering my healing journey. I needed someone to say, "Yes, Favor, it's okay to be angry!" Saying that doesn't make you any less of a Christian. I needed to hear, "I experienced so much self-doubt after my divorce. How on earth can God still love me?" I could relate to that. I wanted to know that my bitter feelings did not make me a bitter person and to know that it was okay to feel the emotions that come with any painful storm. It doesn't make you *any* less of a Christ-believer and it does not lessen His love for you. I received the most healing from books where the author was vulnerable and transparent because it reminded me that we are all human and will all go through storms, but it doesn't change the love that God has for each of us.

As I conclude my own book, I felt led for several months to read Tyler Perry's book, *Higher is Waiting*. As I read it, it became very evident that it was no coincidence. In all the busyness of my life, I somehow managed to read that book in a matter of three days so that certainly had to be God working. I've always been a Tyler Perry fan, but not for the obvious reasons. There are people who you connect with and understand on a spiritual level and, although this is someone who is a celebrity and not running in my circles, I felt his love for Christ even before I read his book. His book confirmed what I've always felt. His story and testimony are beyond amazing, but when a person has a relationship with Jesus, it makes all the sense in the world. We need more Tyler Perry's. His work ethic and what he has accomplished professionally is remarkable, but his love for Jesus and people is what truly makes him an amazing soul.

His book has been a confirmation for what God has been telling me lately. The past few years have been a rollercoaster emotionally. I'm months away from losing a third of my income due to my alimony ending with no clear sight on how to replace it. I'm scared and frustrated yet I'm hopeful and filled with faith. Easy? No, not even a little bit. Doable? Yes. Worth it? Absolutely! God has not let me fail yet and there's no reason to believe He will ever.

I have been working very intentionally from the beginning of my divorce in 2017 to start planting the seeds that will hopefully generate more income for my daughter and me. I started my own personal training business, but soon realized that was not my full calling. It hasn't been wasted time though. My overall goal is motivating and inspiring in all aspects of fitness — physical fitness, spiritual fitness, mental, academic, and professional. I share this because it's important to understand that God will bless your life, but you can't sit by idly without putting in the work. I knew I wanted to be able to provide completely for my daughter, but I also knew God had a purpose for my life. My purpose in the job I had did not bring in the income I needed, which also brought on a lot of stress. This is all part of my overall storm. By continuing to plant seeds, I know that God will bless them and allow those seeds to grow.

I started with the amazing thought planted from God, my mentoring group, Fit For Your Purpose, in January in 2018. The young ladies in my group have truly been a blessing. They remind me all the time how grateful they are for me, but it's really the other way around. I have built strong relationships with each of the ladies in my mentoring group. I'm truly blessed to be in the position I am to speak words of encouragement into their young lives and be that sounding board they need when they need it. I encourage you to seek others out who you can help, especially when you're in a storm. You will be amazed at just how powerful a healer this is.

I started teaching part-time at another university in March of 2019. I was so grateful it was a job I loved, but if I'm being honest, I much rather would have not had to do it. I needed the income, so I did what I had to do. I was grateful it was a job where my daughter could come with me (she didn't mind and actually enjoyed it at times) and we didn't have to spend a lot of time apart. After teaching a full day, you really don't want to gear up again to go teach for another three-four hours. But even in the midst of the tough times, God showed up. He blessed me with a job that opened up other doors for me, allowed me to meet great people, and I only had to teach once a week in person with the rest of the time was online. How's that for a blessing when you're a single parent?

The reason for sharing all of these snapshots of my life over the couple years is to illustrate the realness of God's love, grace, mercy, and forgiveness that will show up despite the storm you're in, have been through, or will go through. I have allowed myself to be broken by God, but only to be rebuilt stronger than ever. Allowing yourself to be broken is not easy. Not even a little bit. Honestly, I didn't know I was being broken until I started coming out of the storm and God revealed this to me. Being broken is beyond painful. However, it's completely necessary if you want to move forward with healing and becoming who God wants you to be.

As I'm completing this book, I'm seeing less rain and more reign. I'm an ordinary person who truly just wants to love Jesus, be a great mom, help people, and live life to my fullest potential. My prayer is that you come away from this book knowing that no matter who you are, where you are, or what you have done, God wants to see you reign in your storm. He will carry you through the storm. He will give you the strength to endure the storm. Through the tears, the heartache, the pain, and shame, our heavenly Father will give you what you need and rebuild you stronger than ever. Allow God to turn that rain into reign! God bless you!

Epilogue

And all of these blessings shall come upon you and overtake you, if you obey the voice of the Lord your God.
--Deuteronomy 28:2 (ESV)

I have felt God's timing and guidance in the entire process of writing this book and adding this epilogue was no different. I felt a push from God that He wanted me to add this epilogue just weeks before releasing my book. I was already in the final stages of publishing my book when the storm of all storms hit for many of us.

Currently, as I start typing this, I sit in my living room with my daughter on a Sunday morning, knowing we will not get up and go to work and school the next day. I will begin teaching classes only online from home and she will be attending her classes in the same format. We were not allowed to attend church in person and our weekend routine of having dinner out at a restaurant had to be postponed.

Social distancing has become our new norm in just a few short weeks. As a society, we're not permitted to gather in large groups and many people have been mandated to work from home. Several states and cities, including the one I live in, have implemented a stay and shelter mandate, which simply means you cannot leave your home unless it's for necessities or to exercise away from others. School has been canceled across the nation. Some children, like my daughter, will participate in online school, but so many other children are not so fortunate.

Children from lower income homes are missing meals that they would normally receive at school, weddings that have been planned way in advance are being canceled, and sadly, most cannot visit their elderly family members because this population is at high risk health wise.

The coronavirus pandemic has singlehandedly caused an unprecedented upheaval of society. Grocery stores have had to place limits on the amount of goods that can be purchased per person. Many stores have limitations on how many people can be in the store at one time and store hours are limited. Restaurants, movie theaters, and gyms are closed. Concerts, plays, sporting events, and college graduations have been canceled. My daughter and I have equated it to living in an apocalyptic time. Writing this feels like I'm describing something out of a movie.

Many individuals cannot go into the office while so many other people are losing their jobs. Parents are having to juggle kids being home all day, with working from home, while trying to figure out how to pay the bills. And this doesn't even begin to include the stressors of those who have been diagnosed with or have a family member who has been diagnosed with or succumbed to the virus. Individuals who have been diagnosed or who may have potentially been exposed to it are mandated to self-quarantine until they are better, which at minimum has been about fourteen days. As I write this, there is presently no cure or vaccine for this virus.

How on earth do we reign in the storm of a pandemic? This is a monumental problem that has affected *every* single person in the United States as well as people around the world. Anxiety is higher, depression rates are more than likely skyrocketing, fear is widespread, and many people are succumbing to the virus.

In spite of the circumstances, God does not want us to have a spirit of fear. I get it. I know. This is a much easier said than done, and this is the *last* thing that people want to hear sometimes. Yet, it's the *first* thing we need to hear. God's word is very clear. *"Do not be anxious about anything, but in every situation, by prayer and petition, with thanksgiving, present your requests to God"* (Philippians 4:6 NIV).

I, like many people, have had a copious amount of time to think and reflect. We have been forced to sit with ourselves and ruminate on what's to come. We can't ignore it and we can't escape it. This pandemic has shifted our very way of life. It is something that will most likely end up in our history books, in talks on economics, and a definite "remember when?" type conversation for decades to come. As I write this, no one knows how long this will last. So, what do we do? How do we adjust? How do we plan when we don't know what we're planning for? These questions are very relevant to the disturbance of life brought on by the coronavirus, but these questions are often asked in *any* storm of life.

The answer to, "how do we plan when we don't know what we're planning for?" is actually simple, and one that you may not want to hear. The answer is this — we don't plan. Now let me clarify for this response. This is not an irresponsible type of a lack of planning. Many areas of our lives require some form of planning. For example, if we have family members coming from out-of-town to stay with us, we must plan for more people in the house. If our child is going off to college, we must plan for their educational expenses. Many of us plan when we want to have families and how many children we want to have.

However, what do we do when we spend more money buying extra food only to find out those family members can't make it? What happens when we get laid off from our job the semester right before our high school senior is due to graduate? What do we do when we have tried for months or even years to start a beautiful family only to be told you cannot conceive? All of the planning in the world won't make us immune to the unexpected changes that will arise in our lives. Life will always throw things our way that will force us to throw all of our planning out the window and find a way to suddenly adjust.

The unpredicted and radical shift in life due to the coronavirus has forced us to take one day at a time, whether we like it or not. Could it be that, just as the Lord tells us in Proverbs 16:9, we can plan what we want but only God can guide our steps? As a society, we are learning the true meaning of taking one day at a time.

Reigning in the Storm

The pandemic has caused the ultimate "time-out" for us as a society. I use this analogy in reference to what is often used with kids to have them stop engaging in unpleasant behavior. A time-out is supposed to force you to sit down and "think" about the poor behavior you were engaged in and hopefully shift to what would be a "better" form of behavior. Please hear me when I say that I am in no way saying the coronavirus is a punishment. The point I'm making is that society has been placed on hold as a result of this virus. We have no choice, but to think about our lives and the direction they're going. One of my prayers is that this time is not wasted for individuals to understand that no matter how hard we try to plan, God is still in control.

A cataclysm of this magnitude should force every individual in society to stop and reflect on what or who we have or haven't made a priority in our lives. Why did we, as a society, need a national crisis to prioritize time with our loved one? The people that we often treat the worse are the ones closest to us. The people that we take for granted, yet expect them to be there for us unconditionally are the people we're now forced to share unlimited and indefinite time with. During this time, a lot of us are irritated because our daily routines have been interrupted. Could this be a lesson in learning not only to adapt, but also to appreciate who and what we have?

I don't believe in wasting pain. Pain *always* has a purpose. Think about it. Even pain in our bodies serves a purpose—it tells us something is wrong. So, what is the purpose of this pandemic? I may not be able to give you a definitive answer on God's plan, but I can say that God gives each of us the ability to have perspective. In any storm in life, we can choose a perspective that is filled with defeat, or we can rise to the occasion and choose a perspective that enables us to keep moving forward.

As a sociologist, I understand all too well that, compared to previous decades, religion has become less significant in our American society. Many people have shifted away from church and religion. And truthfully, many people may have some very valid reasons why they have made this shift. But make no mistake, God is *still* God. Could it be that God needed to desperately get our attention to remind us that He is still in control? He is *still* Lord over everything and Creator of all things.

I'm reminded, as so many of us go through this storm together, of how I personally felt in the middle of the previous storms I described in this book. More times than I can count, I wondered why God was allowing each storm to happen. I knew there was a purpose, but what was it? That is how many people feel today with the pandemic. I'm sure the questions have been asked, "How could a loving, merciful God allow such a catastrophic event to take place in our society?" Sometimes I hear statements such as, "If God is all powerful, He could stop this at any time." God *is* all-powerful and all-knowing, yet that doesn't mean He doesn't care. Quite the contrary. Jeremiah 32:17 states, *"Lord God, with your great power you made the earth and the sky. There is nothing too hard for you to do"* (ERV). The beautiful verses from Psalms 139 reminds us that God has searched us and knows all of our ways and that His knowledge is too wonderful for us to even understand. We have to trust that God knows best, even if we think we do.

Before a pandemic is labeled as such, it usually starts off as an epidemic. One of the meanings of the prefix 'epi' is 'upon.' Most people know an epidemic to be a widespread disease…a disease that is *upon* a distinct population of people. Coronavirus fits this definition. I believe it's no coincidence that I'm writing about an *epi*demic turned pandemic in my *epi*logue. An epilogue is a writing that comes *upon* the end of a book. There was a connection with this for me, so as I was writing, I kept digging and researching and I asked God to reveal it to me.

God wants us to remember something. His blessings will come *upon* us if we call on His name. Deuteronomy 28:2 is very clear about this. In a time where circumstances can easily make us feel unsure, uneasy, and unprepared, we can find an indescribable peace in the One who created us. God did not create us with a spirit of fear! Hear me when I say this — there is **no** storm that is too big for God! No pandemic, no financial circumstance, no bad relationship, no drug, or no sickness. He has called us to REIGN!

My ultimate goal in writing this book was to give hope. I wanted to share my personal storms so others could see that there is sunshine on the other side. You just have to keep going. How do you keep going? By remembering that God will not let you fall. I write this, however, knowing that some of you feel like He has done just that. Maybe you're angry with God because you feel He did let you fall. It's absolutely okay if you feel angry. God created us and every emotion we feel. Nothing surprises Him. He will not love you any less for being angry. He understands.

I pray this book gives you hope no matter what insurmountable storm you may be facing. You may be feeling defeated in some area of your life and that's okay. I just don't want you to stay there. I want this book to be a reminder of God's endless love, mercy, and grace. As I write this out though, I'm reminded of the frequent moments where the words in a book just weren't enough. I needed to hear someone tell me it was going to be alright (and not in a very passive, cliché, sort of way, but I needed to know they actually believed it). More than hearing it from any particular person, I needed and wanted to hear it from God.

Let me be clear that I'm very careful not to speak on God's behalf. However, I do feel that He does speak through people and I know the timing of this book, this epilogue, and all that is happening in our society at this point in time is by no accident. (As I'm typing these words, I was quickly reminded of something I heard Pastor Steven Furtick say once (via YouTube) from his pulpit, *"God's pseudonym is 'coincidence."*) Amen to that! This moment in time that you are reading this book is not by accident. Trust that God is working in your life even as we speak.

God is reminding me that hope is not lost just because we can't feel it. More so than any other time in history, we *have* to lean into the Word of God. I believe that God wants us to know that no matter the size of the storm, He is there. He wants us to know that we can trust Him. I realize that everyone reading this book may not have a personal relationship with Jesus Christ. I have great news for you! The Son of God is waiting to be accepted into your life, so you can have an abundant life in God. This is a free gift to every person walking this earth. It will cost you nothing. The price has already been paid! (Thank you, Jesus!) You will not regret the decision of walking with God and allowing Him to be Head of your life. You have absolutely **nothing** to lose.

If you do have a personal relationship with Jesus Christ, maybe you have been struggling a bit in feeling His presence in your life. Trust that He's been with you the entire time and will continue to walk by your side. Please be reminded of what God says in Isaiah 41:10 in The Message, *"Don't panic. I'm with you. There's no need to fear for I'm your God. I'll give you strength. I'll help you. I'll hold you steady, keep a firm grip on you."*

My heart was disheartened to see that at time when we should have been coming together as a society, many people were angry and placing blame on others. Everyone was pointing the finger at "everyone else." Social psychology will help us to understand that too often, our self-bias kicks in and we think we are not the problem, but it's all the **other**

people around us. Yet often times, we've contributed
in our own way. Due to many people "hoarding"
items, stores were forced to start placing limits on the
number of items individuals could purchase at one
time. Why did we even have to get to that point? I'd
like to believe that we were hoarding in order to help
supply goods to family and friends who may not be
as physically able to make it out of their home. Sadly,
I know that's not the main reason why.

Devastating societal issues (such as a pandemic)
should draw us closer together not push us apart. In
the same fashion, personal storms should draw us
closer to God, not further away. God wants us to
know that in all the instability that life can and will
throw our way, He will never change. He is constant.
Malachi 3:6 (NIV) says, *"I the Lord do not change"* and
Hebrews 13:8 (NIV) reminds us that *"Jesus Christ is
the same, yesterday and today and forever."*

While God has remained and will always be the
same, we change. Our emotions get the best of us
and we want to be in control. The coronavirus
pandemic reminded us that we are *not* in control.
There is one thing, however, that we *are* in control
over. And that is, how we respond to storms. We can
choose to reign, or we can choose to let the rain,
storm clouds, hail, and wind overtake us. We can
choose to say, "God, no matter what, I trust you!" or
we can doubt God and let fear and anxiety consume
us. My prayer is that you choose faith over doubt.
My hope is that you choose peace over fear. And my
goal in writing this book is to allow God to use me to
remind you that no storm is too big for Him.

During the end of 2019, I experienced a lot of stress because of the anticipation of losing income. I dug deeper into my Word and tried to fight hard against the fear and anxiety that kept trying to creep in. I had to be intentional every day about trusting God. I couldn't just rely on my feelings and emotions because they would lead me in the wrong direction every single time. I had to purposefully say out loud, "God, I trust you today." I share this with you because in a time of uncertainty, your emotions can and will get the best of you. If you've never been intentional about taking control over your emotions, now is the time to start.

During this same time period of 2019, God spoke to me a lot about doubt and fear. I was consumed with both. (Little did I know I would be writing about it in a book.) I believed I was trusting God yet, at the same exact time, my stomach was in knots when I counted down the months to when I knew I would be losing income. Because of my somatic symptoms of stress, I started to question myself on whether or not I was truly trusting God.

God doesn't want us to be hard on ourselves. I'm guilty of this. I'm guilty of trying to get it "right." I read all the scriptures on having faith and trusting in God, but sometimes I feel like I will never get to where God wants me to be in my faith journey. If I can be vulnerable and real, no matter how strong I feel my faith is, I sometimes question whether all of this (as in my faith) is worth it. Satan's expertise includes putting those doubts into our minds. He's a master deceiver and guess what? Sometimes we fall for it. I know I have. Can you relate to this?

Fear can do one of two things to us — it can bring out the best in us or it can bring out the worse in us. We've seen this with the coronavirus. We've heard and seen news reports of people hoarding goods from the stores and we've heard of people giving groceries to neighbors. We've heard of people getting into arguments about what a person is buying at the store and we've heard of people sewing masks at no cost for our medical personnel. We've seen people complaining about all the "other" people on social media and still we've seen teachers drive their cars in neighborhoods with signs saying hi and waving to their kids. Let's become people who allow fear to bring out the best in us in our storms.

You may be reading this book in the midst of the coronavirus pandemic, months after life has gotten back to some sense of normalcy, or years after it first originated. It's not often that something happens in society that impacts *every* person in some shape of form. The coronavirus does not discriminate. It doesn't care if you're old or young, Black or White, rich or poor, Christian or Muslim, employed or unemployed. A lot of our choices and in some ways, our freedoms, have been stripped from us, but there's always something positive in a negative. Let me give you a few examples.

We live in a time where technology is a norm, and, in many ways, we've grown to rely on it. Many people have been able to telecommute, which has automatically given them more time with our families. Isn't that something that many of us often complain about—not having enough time for? Yes, colleges and universities have had to transition all classes to online, which may not be ideal for all, but I remain grateful that many of my college students can complete their coursework for the semester and not fall behind in their classes.

Churches all over the United States have had to stop meeting face-to-face, but thanks to technological platforms such as YouTube, Facebook, and Instagram, pastors have been able to livestream their messages. I've even seen a few online where they took questions from viewers and answered them during their sermon—something that does not typically happen during a traditional church service. A local church in the city I live in thought outside the box and did a drive-in church service, where parishioners worshipped from inside their vehicles and the pastor preached from the outside roof of the church! Talk about following Jesus' example!

During my morning runs around my neighborhood, I have seen more people out running or jogging, riding bikes, and my daughter and I even saw someone flying a kite! (Be honest, when's the last time you saw someone flying a kite?) I have seen more kids outside (understandably so) riding bikes, playing with their siblings or family members, or just walking with their parents more than I have seen in quite a long time. My daughter even made a comment to me and said it was nice to see people outside of their homes.

Even with the influx of bad news, there have been news stories that show acts of kindness — many involving people volunteering to help others during a time when any contact with others could be detrimental to one's own health. I've read about strangers sewing medical masks for our nurses and doctors, and people donating the extra groceries they have to elderly couples. Kindness and support always win in the face of adversity.

I know just how difficult it can be to see the beautiful, bright, sunny sky when you're in the eye of the storm. As I write this, I'm reminded of a former student of mine who had just lost her younger brother to an untimely death just a month or so prior to the coronavirus pandemic. I reached out to her regularly to see how she and her family were doing, but sometimes it was just so difficult to come up with the right words to say. What do you say to someone who feels beaten, broken, and battered? This, my friend, is also the question I have asked myself so often while writing this book.

I leave you with this. Whether it's life's personal storms or a pandemic, the essentials we need can be hard to come by. During a pandemic, this may include food, household essentials, or even income. On a personal level, the essentials may include sleep, eating, happiness, good health, and peace. During these dry seasons, God will *never* leave us or forsake us. Deuteronomy 31:8 says, *"The Lord himself goes before you and will be with you; he will never leave you nor forsake you. Do not be afraid; do not be discouraged"* (NIV).

God will not leave us to fend for ourselves. He will come alongside of us and help carry us through even the darkest of storms. I know that it's not always easy. That's okay. I get that for some people the thought of there being a God who takes care of our every need just seems too implausible. A relationship with Jesus Christ is the *one* thing that will help you to move forward, even if it's just one step at a time. You can get through this. You **will** get through this!

We do not have to wait until our circumstances change in order to rejoice on the inside. Habakkuk 3:17 illustrates this very thing by stating, "*the fig trees may not bud*" or "*the fields produce no food.*" In today's time we may equate these to "our bank accounts having no money" or "no food in our pantries to eat." Verse eighteen brings hope by stating, *"Yet I will rejoice in the Lord, I will be joyful in God my Savior."* Jesus will give you what you need in order that you may rejoice, no matter how much you have or how much you need. You, my dear friend, will '**R**ejoice **E**ven **I**n **G**reat **N**eed." You will R.E.I.G.N!

About the Author

For ten years, she was a stay-at-home-mom. At the age of twenty-eight, Favor Campbell went back to college to complete her bachelor's degree in communications then continued on to complete her master's degree in sociology, both from the University of Texas at San Antonio (UTSA). She is a full-time adjunct sociology professor at UTSA, and she teaches part-time at Park University. In 2017, Favor started her own personal training and wellness business called JFit29 and, in 2018, she started her mentoring group called Fit For Your Purpose. A devoted follower of Jesus Christ, her Christian faith is what has been her anchor in navigating through life. Favor is a single mom to her daughter, Jadyn, and resides in San Antonio, TX.

For more information, go to JFit29.com